This readable book includes astute analysis and practical tools developed by leading specialists with much experience of fixing teams. It is welcome and timely, especially as there are so many work teams that are dysfunctional. Fixing them would benefit all concerned.

—**Professor Greg J. Bamber,** Monash Business School, Monash University

In today's busy workplace, the need to work productively and harmoniously with others is critical, but not always the reality. *Fix Your Team* explores the common dysfunctions that can derail your team's effectiveness, and provides practical solutions to move your team dynamic from dysfunctional to functional. Make some time to *Fix Your Team*.

—**Dermot Crowley,** author of *Smart Work* and *Smart Teams* and founder of Adapt Productivity

Fix Your Team is a very well organized, step-by-step guide for anyone who wants to improve their workplace and team dynamics, regardless of the size of their organization. From toxic personalities and reluctant or abrasive managers, to downsizing and overtime, the authors tackle every imaginable issue and break them down into manageable bites of what to do. Rose Bryant-Smith and Grevis Beard pack decades of experience into this very practical guidebook.

—**Bill Eddy,** training director, High Conflict Institute, and author of 5 *Types of People Who Can Ruin Your Life: Identifying and Dealing with Narcissists, Sociopaths and Other High-Conflict Personalities*

A wonderfully practical and informative tool for leaders, with helpful examples and case studies that will really guide you through the difficult scenarios we see on a daily basis, not just the theory!

—**Rebecca Fraser,** Head of Human Resources, Energy, ˉnergyAustralia

D1283606

Finally! A book that addresses the most commonplace issues impacting team dynamics and effectiveness...and delivered with logic and humour. Rose and Grevis are to be congratulated on clearly identifying both the problems AND the solutions.

—**Cath Gillard,** Executive Director, People & Culture, Australian Red Cross Blood Service

In today's competitive environment, organisations need to bring out the best in everyone. *Fix Your Team* is a definitive guide for all those on the front line—managers, human resources, risk, legal and other internal advisors—to get employees working with, and not against, each other. With actionable guidance on building buy-in, executing the strategy and staying the course in tough times, *Fix Your Team* is an essential read.

—**Christina Gillies,** independent company director and Chair of the Victorian Council of the International Women's Forum

There is a lot of preaching about the value of teams at work – but it's not always backed up with practice. Here's a book that locates the most common problems and helps you and your team fix them. A clearly written handbook that will help you and your colleagues realise their true potential.

—**Rob Goffee,** Emeritus Professor, Organisational Behaviour, London Business School

Fix Your Team offers a comprehensive guide to the problems faced by those managing a team. The authors' experience and expertise are apparent in the detailed analysis of underlying problems and practical advice to resolve them. Every manager will find value in these pages.

—**Nick Grant,** Director of Human Resources, Australia, K&L Gates

This book will be a critical read for all managers and professionals looking to build a thriving team. It's easy to find a book to tell you how to build a great team, but there are not many that so effectively and pragmatically help you to eliminate the dysfunction and barriers that will prevent you from even starting to thrive! Read it all, or dip into it when you see dysfunction—either way, you will find real and practical help.

— **Aaron Lamers,** Human Resources Director Northern
Europe, General Mills

Managing your team has just become a whole lot easier with this book. *Fix Your Team* is a compelling guide to realising your team's full potential. The authors advance specific team goals and offer a myriad of suggestions, including fun team activities, on how to achieve this. This book is a must-have reference for all team managers.

— **Isabel Metz,** Professor of Organisational Behaviour,
Melbourne Business School

A must read for anyone despairing of the dysfunctional team they have joined, inherited or hired. *Fix Your Team* is the practical guide for leaders, managers and employees that provides realistic solutions to seemingly impossible team dysfunctionality. The Fix Your Team Toolkit will help you shift the dysfunction and build team morale, values and good behaviours.

— **Kimberle**y **Poynton,** Head of Human Resources,
Ivanhoe Grammar School

When teams work well, they work very very well, and when they don't, they are horrid. If you ever need help with improving your team's dynamics, then this book is the one for you. It is the 'one stop shop' for unearthing what's going wrong, identifying the ways forward, and implementing the necessary solutions.

— **Chris Roussos,** Executive Director, People & Corporate
Support, St Vincent's Hospital, Melbourne

Fix Your Team is the tool that many team leaders have been wanting. For many years, I have written and spoken about organisational culture. Every team, no matter how big or small, has a culture. The team leader is pivotal in setting in that culture. Where can a team leader start in assessing and improving the team's culture? Reading *Fix Your Team* is the ideal starting point.

— **Neville Tiffen,** specialist consultant in business integrity, corporate governance and compliance, member OECD Secretary-General's high level advisory group on integrity and anti-corruption

Teams outperform individuals when they work well together! *Fix Your Team* identifies common team dysfunctions then offers 14 insightful, tailored and specific tools to overcome them. Anyone on any team would be well served by accessing these insights.

— **Dave Ulrich,** Rensis Likert Professor, Ross School of Business, University of Michigan

FIX YOUR TEAM

The tools you need to rebuild relationships, address conflict and stop destructive behaviours

Rose Bryant-Smith
Grevis Beard

WILEY

First published in 2018 by John Wiley & Sons Australia, Ltd
42 McDougall St, Milton Qld 4064

Office also in Melbourne

Typeset in 11/13.5pt Palatino LT Std

© John Wiley & Sons Australia, Ltd 2018

The moral rights of the authors have been asserted

A catalogue record for this book is available from the National Library of Australia

Cover design by Wiley

Cover image and internal illustrations © Flipser/Shutterstock

Printed in Singapore by C.O.S. Printers Pte Ltd

10 9 8 7 6 5 4 3 2 1

Disclaimer

Although based on aspects of actual complaints, conflicts and team dysfunction we have resolved in our professional work, no character, situation or organisation described in this book represents any real person, situation or organisation. The contents of this book are provided as general information only. We recommend seeking advice from a qualified lawyer before acting on any matter with legal implications.

The material in this publication is of the nature of general comment only, and does not represent professional advice. It is not intended to provide specific guidance for particular circumstances and it should not be relied on as the basis for any decision to take action or not take action on any matter which it covers. Readers should obtain professional advice where appropriate, before making any such decision. To the maximum extent permitted by law, the authors and publisher disclaim all responsibility and liability to any person, arising directly or indirectly from any person taking or not taking action based on the information in this publication.

To the team at Worklogic. Every day you demonstrate accountability, integrity, confidence, wisdom and joy. Every day you innovate and collaborate to build happy, healthy, productive workplaces across Australia. Worklogic is the best team we know.

CONTENTS

Contents

ABOUT THE AUTHORS

Rose Bryant-Smith is an in-demand workplace consultant and company director. With a background in employment law, ethics and leadership, she has a deep understanding of workplace dynamics and what makes people tick. Rose is passionate about building productive and happy workplaces, where everyone can thrive.

Grevis Beard's career over the last twenty years has included legal, advocacy and consulting roles. His advice is sought on the full gamut of workplace behaviour issues, conundrums and conflicts. A self-diagnosed extrovert, Grevis is a popular speaker on the conference circuit.

Together Rose Bryant-Smith and Grevis Beard co-founded and lead Worklogic, a respected workplace advisory firm. Worklogic works with employers to prevent and minimise the impact of inappropriate conduct in the workplace, and to build a positive culture. Worklogic's client list includes major companies, government departments, non-profits and other good employers across Australia.

For more information on Worklogic, visit www.worklogic.com.au

ACKNOWLEDGEMENTS

Our heartfelt gratitude goes to our incredible families, who support us to grow and to thrive. We also thank our clients—experienced managers, workplace relations advisers, law firm partners and other experts—who provided sage advice and helpful feedback on this manuscript.

INTRODUCTION
Don't worry! You can 'fix your team'

Working in a dysfunctional team is frustrating and stressful. No one wants to show up every day to a team that is constantly distracted by in-fighting, dragging each other down, disrupting one another's performance, performing poorly, or engaging in unethical behaviour. At Worklogic we hear story after story of employees who feel sick with dread when they arrive at work in the morning, who despair as the team's productive efforts are undermined, and who feel like they spend more time working on the team's issues than getting the real work done. This sort of dysfunction has an impact on team members, managers, leaders, and service functions such as human resources, risk, legal and compliance.

Team dysfunction quickly becomes visible to the broader organisation. Complaints, gossip, staff turnover and transfers out of the group are all signs that things are not going well. The team's tangible results also suffer. This can reflect poorly on the manager of the team, whose reputation, fairly or unfairly, will inevitably be affected. This is not something the organisation can afford to ignore.

Team dysfunction can have a huge personal and psychological impact. Whatever your role, you may feel stressed, anxious and preoccupied, and confused about what is going on. You may be unsure how to go about fixing things and be worried that, even if you 'do something', team communication, behaviour and morale could keep getting worse.

If you're working in, managing or advising a dysfunctional team, you will see firsthand the destructive impact of team dysfunction on productivity, cooperation, innovation, communication, output and morale, as well as the flow-on effects on profitability and customer satisfaction.

If this sounds familiar to you, you are not alone! From decades of experience in helping employers to identify and address team dysfunction, we know that managers and supervisors are often frustrated by a lack of time, experience, resources or good advice on how to deal with these problems. Meanwhile, employees working in the team feel powerless and fearful of the consequences for their job security if they speak up.

That's why we wrote this book. Treat it like a workplace lifebuoy: keep it safe and always within reach.

If you are a manager, by applying the Fix Your Team Toolkit of interventions you will demonstrate leadership skills that will help you to cement (or if necessary salvage) the respect and trust of your reports and your colleagues. You'll demonstrate that you are 'on top of the problem' and have the skills to handle tricky situations in your team. Rather than go to your own supervisor or to Human Resources with the problem ('My team is a mess and I don't know what to do about it'), you'll demonstrate insight and good judgement by presenting the challenge, the solution and the business case for the remedial intervention in a professional and credible way.

If you work in a service function such as Human Resources or Risk and Compliance, a core part of your role is to advise on tricky workplace situations. You know that dysfunctional teams can create havoc in the organisation. Problem teams that are left to their own devices only become more problematic.

Entrenched problems rarely solve themselves, and they have impacts that are far broader than the personal consequences for individual team members. The risks arising from bad behaviour and poor team functioning include:

- legal claims such as bullying, sexual harassment and discrimination

- occupational health and safety risks and compensation claims

- absenteeism, and consequent increased pressure on remaining team members

- allegations of misconduct, which can place additional obligations on the organisation under industrial agreements, policies and procedures

- employee complaints

- reputational impacts if problems become public

- employee turnover and resignations of good staff

- the involvement of employment commissions and health and safety regulators

- in public sector agencies and highly regulated industries, involvement of the ombudsman or anti-corruption agencies.

Team members, meanwhile, deserve better than to have to tolerate dysfunction, disputes and disappointment affecting *one-third of their waking hours* (for full-time workers). Life is too short to spend it in a toxic work environment! One of the worst impacts for employees is a sense of hopelessness, the feeling that you are stuck: there is nothing you can do to change your situation, but you can't afford to change jobs. *Fix Your Team* offers real, practical hope to team members, as well as team managers and advisers. Everyone can influence a team's morale, values and behaviours, so they can all look forward to going to work again.

The guided approach we outline in this book can be applied by anyone who is working in, managing or advising a dysfunctional team. Whether you are a team member, in a service function, a team manager or a more senior executive with a dysfunctional team in your portfolio, this book will help. It will teach you how to identify dysfunction in your team, understand what is really going on, work out what to do about it and get everyone back to work. We will help you to:

- develop confidence in your analysis of team problems
- learn what tools are available to shift a destructive, inefficient or unethical dynamic
- identify which tool will work best (including the best use of your resources)
- develop the business case for resourcing an intervention, and win support from the top (including budget) to take action
- build the buy-in and respect of your team members.

There are incredible benefits to be gained for the team and the organisation in tackling head-on the problems that are holding your team back. *Fix Your Team* will help you to:

- significantly improve productivity
- increase your colleagues' engagement with the work and with the organisation's mission
- create an environment that supports employee wellbeing
- increase job satisfaction
- improve innovation through increased mutual trust and openness to new ways of thinking
- maximise the opportunity for everyone to bring their best to the job, thereby improving overall performance
- create a happier working environment for everyone.

If you are a manager, you will also demonstrate your commitment to productivity, genuine care for your employees and a healthy working environment. You will earn greater respect from your direct reports and peers and from senior managers, and demonstrate that the company values are real and not just marketing spin.

HOW TO USE THIS BOOK

This book is structured to be used flexibly and practically. Part I sets out 12 common situations that cause team dysfunction and identifies some of the key problems you may be dealing with. We have also provided you with case studies based on real-life scenarios from workplaces across the world to demonstrate what team dysfunctions look like. Once you have a better feel for what's going on in your own workplace, read Part II to identify which tools you need to apply. These tools are arranged in themes, according to the outcome you are trying to achieve.

These tested strategies include practical exercises you can use to implement change in your team. In each case we provide a description of the tool, what you need to do to implement it, and tips and traps to be aware of as you do so. Some of the tools you can implement yourself; others may need the involvement of Human Resources or an external expert.

It can be tricky to navigate the politics of your organisation to gain the understanding, buy-in and resources you'll need. Part III explains how to build a plan, a business case and support in your organisation for the interventions you have chosen.

Addressing team dysfunction can be tough. You will be implementing change, having difficult conversations and telling some people what they don't want to hear. The final chapter, 'Buckle up!', sets out four strategies you can use to remain effective and stay sane as you set about fixing your team.

While your team is getting back on track, we're here to help. Keep in touch and access additional help and advice by subscribing at www.fix-your-team.com.

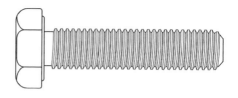

PART I
WHAT IS GOING ON?

Before you can apply the right tools to get your team back on track, you first need to identify what's going wrong. You need to:

- recognise the symptoms of the dysfunction/s that are occurring in your team

- understand what conflict, conduct or cultural issues are causing problems, noting where there is more than one

- think through the problems from the perspective of your colleagues in the team. What is their lived experience of the team right now? What is driving their behaviours? What are they trying to achieve? How do they want things to be different?

Don't worry if you feel a little overwhelmed as you begin to diagnose the issues. The chapters in part I are designed to help you. We will set out the 12 most common dysfunctions that we have seen in workplaces across Australia and overseas over the past 20 years.

The Symptoms box at the start of each chapter in Part I lists the behaviours that commonly manifest when a team is in the grip of that particular dysfunction. Do any of those symptoms look familiar? You may very quickly recognise a dysfunction that you and your team are experiencing. Keep reading and you'll learn how and why that problem arises, and how it affects team functioning.

Don't stop when you identify one dysfunction your team is experiencing. There may be one or a variety of issues, which may be distinct or enmeshed together. In our experience, it's rare that only one specific problem affects a team over a long period of time. Usually a team in crisis is facing two or three challenges, such as an unassertive manager, confusion over accountabilities and values, and a toxic personality who is taking advantage of the situation. Review all 12 dysfunctions to determine whether more than one is present in your team.

After identifying the problems your team is facing, Part II will guide you through some further thinking, as you progress towards choosing the right interventions for you.

Chapter 1

GOSSIP CULTURE
Cruel conversations

SYMPTOMS

- Some colleagues are conducting spiteful conversations in which they mock and denigrate others.

- What might have started as harmless banter in the lunch-room, or constructive speculation in challenging times, now has people delighting in others' misfortunes, true or fabricated.

- Cliques are excluding and isolating individuals—socially, professionally or both.

- As the gossip spreads, untrue rumours have started to damage a colleague's professional reputation.

- Gossip spreads to social media platforms.

WHAT'S GOING ON

It's human to want to understand situations, read the play of social activity and recognise the motivations of others. We like to guess at what's going on, and, in our less honourable moments, we may feel smug satisfaction when people we envy or dislike are struggling. Gossip exists in many workplaces, and it can be destructive.

What is gossip?

The positive sharing of information can be healthy. Constructive speculation about what's going on in the company, "building social connections with colleagues, discussion of who might get that sought-after promotion—these conversations are quite natural. As humans, we try to make sense of what's happening around us, even when we have little information on which to base our understanding. Whether out of competition, curiosity or a genuine wish to see our colleagues succeed, we're inherently interested in what other people are doing.

If the speculation is negative and seeks to drag someone else down, that's a very different story. This is gossip: nasty, inflammatory and potentially embarrassing to the target.

Gossiping employees select isolated pieces of information (facts) and turn them into something bigger (speculation). We've all heard it: exaggeration, embellishment and rumours. Will our co-worker get fired? Who did what to whom at the end-of-year party? What's really happening in this or that colleague's life? Many of us have overheard sensational and salacious tales about who has a drinking problem, who is having an affair, drug addiction, financial trouble, and what questionable leverage Kaylene must have with the CEO to have won that promotion.

The problem is that such reality TV–style dramas are often embellished, unreliable and disruptive. Gossips who fabricate juicy tales when they should be working are often incredibly distracting to their co-workers. Sharing personal, private information, whether or not it is true, is inappropriate and potentially destructive.

Motivations of gossips

Gossips can be driven by social ambition, self-worth issues, jealousy, spite, mischief or plain old boredom. Some gossips spread rumours to fill the void of a quiet period at work, while others spread gossip deliberately and strategically to gain an advantage over others.

One consequence of gossiping (that the gossips themselves usually don't seem to understand or care about) is that gossips are never trusted. Only other gossips and clueless hangers-on will share information with such people.

Gossip can breach legal standards

At its heart, gossip is a power play used to harm and disempower others. Far from 'harmless', it often amounts to bullying others. Under Australian workplace laws, bullying at work occurs when a person or a group of people *repeatedly* behaves *unreasonably* towards a worker or a group of workers, and the behaviour creates *a risk to health and safety*. Bullying can involve, for example: aggressive or intimidating conduct; belittling or humiliating comments; spreading malicious rumours; teasing, practical jokes or 'initiation ceremonies'; exclusion from work-related events; unreasonable work expectations, including too much work, or work beyond a worker's skill level; displaying offensive material; or pressure to behave in an inappropriate manner.

Negative, targeted and ongoing gossip is, at its heart, a pattern of unreasonable conduct towards a colleague. Gossips use information and misinformation to harm, disempower and exclude others.

Sometimes, gossip includes sexual content and innuendo, or maligning colleagues for engaging in sexual conduct (actual or invented). This can contribute to a sexualised culture and can even amount to *sexual harassment*: unwelcome conduct of a sexual nature.

Gossip can be a symptom or tool of resistance to change, or rejection of accountability. Malicious rumours can be used to undermine, deter or marginalise the manager who is trying to effect change. Gossip can also be about fear or suspicion of outsiders—for example, false statements being made about the beliefs, practices or lifestyle of a stakeholder from a different cultural background (see chapter 7).

Gossip thrives when information is lacking

Aristotle famously said that nature abhors a vacuum, postulating that any space or void would immediately fill with life. Gossip loves silence, filling it with vague information and speculation. Misinformation will thrive when no one in the workplace really knows what's going on. Employees who don't trust their manager or who lack information will *make things up* to fill in the blanks. A false answer, to them, is better than no answer at all.

This means that in times of change or upheaval, such as during restructures, gossip can run riot. In these circumstances, employees quite naturally feel fearful and insecure and seek answers, while the organisation's leaders cannot answer every question, perhaps because not all the information is available yet. Gossips then step in to fill the information void.

IMPACT ON THE TEAM

Gossip can disrupt and damage:

- interpersonal relationships
- the motivation and morale of the team overall
- the systems of work and how employees work together (avoidance and missed opportunities to collaborate)
- productivity
- employee engagement and retention (high-performing employees, feeling either distracted or undermined, seek work elsewhere).

If the gossip spreads to social media platforms, the negativity and criticisms are even more public. These forums are less controlled and far more visible to the outside world, which ramps up the potential risks to the individuals and the employer. Social media creates the perfect environment for gossip to flourish, as the following case study illustrates.

CASE STUDY
FACEBOOK GOSSIP AFTER THE PARTY

The Christmas party at signage company Hancock Signature is always a raucous event. After this year's party, Zara posted some photos of the party on Facebook, including one of machine operator Spyros and Leila, a temp. Underneath the photo, Zara commented, 'Love is in the air'. The photo attracted multiple likes and additional comments alluding to a relationship between Spyros and Leila and suggesting that Leila had been drinking excessively at the party.

The following week in the office, the gossip is rife. Spyros is furious. He is happily married and was talking to Leila to make her feel part of the party, as she was new to the office. Leila, who is a teetotaller for religious reasons, is upset as well. She had been brought in to assist Zara with her work and she wonders whether Zara is trying to intimidate her. She goes to HR to ask what she can do.

You can see from this example how easily gossip can spread. Complaints of sexual harassment and bullying have arisen when gossips have speculated about an affair, that an employee 'slept their way to the top' or that a team member 'got fired from their last job for fraud'.

In these ways gossip creates a toxic culture of distrust in:

- the manager. *My boss is so weak. She's not calling out the bad behaviour that's dragging us down! Doesn't she realise that the gossips are undermining her too?*

- each other. *If they are gossiping about Leila, what are they saying about me?*

- the organisation. *They say their values are respect, honesty and collaboration. What a joke!*

Of course, the people who are most affected by gossip are the targets themselves. Gossip can tear down their reputations, disrupt their careers and distract them from the tasks at hand. It causes anger, embarrassment and shame. They waste their time focusing on social dynamics rather than on productive work. Rumours and fabrications can be so inflammatory that they push a person to quit.

A gossip culture within a team is hard for the supervisor to manage, as it's difficult to intervene in one-on-one 'social' conversations, so they can spend enormous amounts of time trying to manage the fallout.

Chapter 2

UNPROFESSIONAL CONDUCT

When bad behaviour goes unchecked

SYMPTOMS

- Every year, the Christmas party for the sales department is the HR manager's nightmare, as it includes a prize for 'sexiest new recruit' and an alcohol-fuelled midnight swim in Sydney Harbour.

- A core group of employees deliberately excludes, ignores and 'freezes out' other employees, particularly from meetings, office social functions and group emails.

- For years, an employee has habitually used sexual innuendo in office banter and emails, and boasted of their sexual conquests during the weekends.

- 'Practical jokes' in the office include placing condoms on a colleague's desk, regularly stealing lunches from the fridge, or moving colleagues' personal items around the office.

- Casual discrimination and micro-aggressions—such as, 'Why can't they all go home to their own country?' or 'You can't invite a woman out for coffee these days without breaching the sexual harassment policy'—are common in the workplace.

- Employees are posting derogatory comments about each other and about the company on social media.

WHAT'S GOING ON

Written policies and standards of professional behaviour exist in most workplaces. Despite this, when you're having a bad day, it can be difficult to mask your feelings and keep your negativity, anger, anxiety or frustrations to yourself.

These 'bad days' become a problem when they keep happening. When the bad days are causing hurt and disruption to other members of the team, and the accepted standards of behaviour are slipping, a nasty culture starts to develop. This happens when repeated bad behaviour goes unchecked.

It looks like this. No one says anything when Kath makes another racist joke. No one speaks up when Terry suggests that everyone leave at 3 pm for another boozy Thursday afternoon at the pub and implies that anyone who stays behind is a 'pussy'. No one intervenes when shouting is heard through Antonia's office door, for the third time this week.

Understanding workplace culture

The culture of a team or organisation defines boundaries for behaviours and relationships, provides incentives and disincentives, and binds the members of the group to one another. A vital element is the shared beliefs and values of the group, which determine what is (and is not) acceptable, expected and encouraged behaviour. Culture reflects what we are really striving for and guides how we go about achieving our goals. Culture is *what it feels like* to work in this group each day. People's experience of workplace culture is predominantly local (the immediate team), and the biggest influence is their immediate line manager.

Workplace cultures are as varied as the people who work in them, and are influenced by the industry, the type of work that the team is engaged in, the broader values of the organisation and other factors. To achieve their goals, organisations may strive to cultivate a culture of 'winning', 'compassion', 'competition' or 'continuous improvement'.

'Culture eats strategy for breakfast', said business management guru Peter Drucker. Culture is critically important in a workplace and contributes to—or detracts from—the long-term success of both the team and the organisation.

Workplace culture over time

Workplace culture develops and evolves over time, building with each action that is (and is not) taken by leaders, managers, staff and other stakeholders. With each sexist remark that is tolerated in the workplace, the culture becomes a fraction more misogynist. With each racist 'joke', the culture becomes a little less merit-based and inclusive. The rituals that humiliate certain staff confirm the power of others and contribute to a culture of intolerance.

On the other hand, workplace culture can be influenced for the better relatively quickly. Every time someone blocks the telling of a racist joke, intervenes when someone raises their voice, or objects to dangerous behaviour, the culture shifts again.

The 'little things' can make a big difference to workplace culture, because they all add up. Every action that is allowed in the workplace helps define what is and is not acceptable, and confirms everyone's understanding of the values that underpin how we work together. Every interaction, decision and action is a values marker, and far more telling than the 'official' values as listed on the organisation's website.

Recognise that it's hard for team members to intervene

Here is one realisation you might find empowering, whatever your role. If your team is suffering from a culture of toxic behaviour, *you are not the only person in the team who finds it offensive.* Even if no one else is speaking up and objecting, it's likely others are as disturbed and insulted as you are.

Why don't other people in the team speak up? To understand the bystander effect, we need to recognise that humans are 'programmed' to avoid potentially dangerous situations. When we encounter unusual and possibly threatening behaviour by others, we exercise extreme caution. This automatic reluctance to intervene stems from a desire to avoid harm to ourselves, but when others are present and no one intervenes, it contributes to the bystander effect. In fact, the more observers there are, the smaller the chance of any one person intervening, because of the diffusion of responsibility ('everyone assumes that someone else will step in').

Consider a group email sent by an employee to a number of others, which is mocking and critical of a colleague but leaves that colleague out of the email loop. Let's assume you receive the email and the criticised employee is your friend. What do you do? What if the employee is not your friend? Would your response be different?

When there's a poor culture characterised by unprofessional conduct such as racism, disrespect or inappropriate risk-taking, and no one does anything about it, those who remain silent are almost as culpable as those who are behaving badly. This is particularly true of those who are in positions of authority, who have a big influence on workplace culture, as we can see in the following case study.

CASE STUDY
A DINOSAUR REFUSES TO BECOME EXTINCT

Over time, Blackmount Engineering's workforce has been changing. Taking advantage of more skilled migrants and the higher number of female engineering graduates, the workplace is becoming more diverse. This doesn't sit well with Steve, who has been a mid-level manager for decades. In various ways,

Steve is 'pushing back' and trying to disempower people in the workplace whom he perceives to be challenging the status quo (part-timers, millennials, women, LGBTI staff and people who had trained overseas). He likes to disparage any modern thinking as 'political correctness gone mad'. According to Steve, people who don't laugh at his jokes are 'snowflakes' and 'pansies'.

On paper, Steve reports to Ari, a senior manager. The reality is that Steve is close to John, the owner of Blackmount, and John has overturned Ari's management decisions a few times in the past six months.

After Steve's latest sexist outburst in a meeting, Ari says, 'That's just Steve. He doesn't know any better. He's a good bloke really.' Ari doesn't really believe this. He is just afraid of taking Steve on. The company owner has tolerated Steve's destructive 'banter' for years, and many other staff seem to find Steve funny and harmless. Despite his reservations, Ari pretends to laugh at Steve's 'jokes' and hopes that no one will make a complaint. After yet another offensive run-in with Steve in the tearoom, valued engineer Jasmine comes to Ari to resign. She has accepted a job with one of Blackmount's competitors.

In this example, Ari has become complicit in Steve's nasty conduct by minimising the consequences of his behaviour for the team. Some managers we speak with find it difficult to know where to draw the line: *What behaviour should I act on, what should I ignore?* They are reluctant to intervene because they don't want to be seen as nagging, nitpicking or interfering unnecessarily in employees' personal interactions. They don't want to be seen as a killjoy, by not allowing any 'fun' at work. Further, they fear that by intervening they may be perceived as taking sides, or even make the situation worse for the employees who are subject to the bad behaviour. These concerns are all natural—and very common among bystanders! But by doing nothing, you are allowing the bad behaviour to continue and, in fact, you are tacitly condoning it.

This isn't a time to stick your head in the sand and avoid conflict. Action is required. There is always something you can do to nudge the culture of your team in the right direction.

Bad behaviour online

The proliferation of technology in all aspects of life has led to unprecedented disclosures and freedom of expression and the casualisation of written communication. The fact that many colleagues are connected on social media and via text message outside work as well as at work means that poor behaviour won't always just happen within the four walls of the office.

Technology has made communication much quicker and easier, but it is also more informal and relaxed. Many people forget that content they post on social media doesn't 'disappear' during work hours. It is there 24/7. If colleagues are 'friends' on social media, the post is published and accessible to them during work hours. Some people in your team may have different ideas about privacy and what is appropriate to share on social media. This means that bad behaviour *and workplace culture* can play out online.

IMPACT ON THE TEAM

Bad behaviour that goes unchecked will affect employees differently. Employees who are subjected to disrespectful, offensive and humiliating behaviour may avoid social interactions at work and 'shut down' in group situations. Some may lose focus, feel drained of energy or suffer a loss of confidence. Productivity, discretionary effort, morale and attendance may be affected too. You may end up with an employee who is physically present, but who is distracted at best and simply unable to concentrate on their work, at worst.

Withdrawal—both socially and professionally—is very common. You may find that a team member is keeping their head down in meetings, avoiding work interactions that are not mandatory and taking fewer risks.

Unchecked poor behaviour has a flow-on effect even for those who are not directly involved. Others in the team may be wishing the behaviour would stop but be unsure how to help. Some will have a sinking feeling that *I could be next*, while others may have resigned themselves to fate: *This is the way things are around here. Nothing will change.* If you have found that bad behaviour is going unchecked and damaging the team culture, know that *change is possible*.

Chapter 3

TOXIC PERSONALITIES
One Bad Apple can rot the whole barrel

SYMPTOMS

- Someone in the team (the Bad Apple) often bails you up in the tearoom with a tale of woe or injustice. They talk about how terrible a recent managerial decision was, or describe an 'unfair' situation in minute detail, offering no solutions and making no attempt to understand the situation better.

- The Bad Apple often tries to get you to agree with them and take their side. You feel manipulated and wonder what their agenda is.

- One person commonly makes negative and sarcastic comments in meetings, such as 'I can't see how that is going to work' or 'Yet more management-speak'.

- Eye-rolling, sighing and folded arms—the Bad Apple's body language screams disrespect, defiance and negativity.

- Even when a manager is genuinely trying to effect changes that will support the work quality, client or customer experience, team functioning or innovation, and doing so skilfully, the Bad Apple tries to undermine their efforts.

Note: We are not referring in this chapter to people suffering from a mental health condition or a personal crisis that temporarily affects how they behave at work. Those situations are examined in the following chapter.

WHAT'S GOING ON

We've all been in a situation—in our family, friendship group or workplace—where one person seems to undermine everyone's enjoyment of good things that are going on, and exploits any opportunity to dampen the mood. They are the Bad Apple that can rot the whole barrel.

Their personality seems to drive them to see malicious intent and inadequacy in everyone, everywhere. They won't accept that their colleagues could be genuinely well intentioned, capable and deserving of respect. They are the negative and undermining element in the team.

Some Bad Apples are unaware of the negative impact they have on their colleagues; others derive a sense of pleasure from creating chaos. Some Bad Apples engage in obviously destructive behaviour; others work more subtly behind the scenes, nibbling away like a termite at the healthy foundations of the team, the damage remaining undetected until late in the piece. Either way, they suck time and energy from those around them. Here's an example of a sophisticated Bad Apple at work.

CASE STUDY
TRICKY TEA BREAK

Karim and Jenny work in a commercial laundry that services the regional hospital, local hotels and other businesses. Jenny often

---

finds Karim on breaks and sits next to him, treating him as the audience for her tales of woe. She regales him with stories of injustice, unfairness in decisions about work opportunities, and conspiracies around what their managers are planning. One day, Jenny says, 'Can you believe what Drew said in the team meeting yesterday? He's so incompetent it's embarrassing. It's incredible that he was made permanent before Bella. It just shows that in this company you need to suck up to the right people. Don't you think?'

Karim is wary of disagreeing with her, fearing that he himself will become the subject of a future reputational attack. Instead he says 'Hmm' a lot, hoping she will go away. Jenny goes on, 'Someone should raise this with management and complain. You are as experienced as Bella and you got overlooked too.'

Later that week, Karim hears that Jenny has told their manager that he was complaining about Drew, when he had done no such thing! The manager then takes Karim aside to talk about not undermining others, and the company values of integrity and honesty. He is outraged when he learns a week later that Jenny has been describing him as 'The Underminer' to the rest of the team.

Psychologists and those working in the field, such as lawyer and mediator Bill Eddy, have characterised these types of behaviours as 'high conflict'. Others call them 'toxic'. People with toxic personalities may be believable at first and may be superficially charming. They are unable to recognise their own contribution to the problem and respond very poorly to criticism. People with toxic personalities are commonly:

- **temperamental**. They have little control over their emotions. They lash out at and project their feelings on others, convinced that others are causing their discontent.

- **always the 'victim'.** Colleagues often empathise with the Bad Apple's problems initially. The Bad Apple is very good at feeling sorry for themselves and manipulating others to take pity on them. Furiously rejecting any personal responsibility for their actions, they defend their perspective and never apologise (as everything is always someone else's fault). Rather than trying to respond constructively to a challenge, they relish the opportunity to suffer.

- **manipulative.** Using a façade of friendship, cooperation or collegiality, manipulators con others into a false sense of security, then take advantage. Their goal is to get people to do what they want them to do. They seek attention, approval and compliance from others. Rather than working with you to reach an amicable conclusion, they maintain control of conversations. Their tactics can include flitting between topics, being vague and arbitrary, and drilling down to irrelevant detail.

- **inconsistent.** Bad Apples use surprise and confusion, changing tactics, perspectives, emotional states and behaviour to keep others off guard. It can be hard to anticipate how Bad Apples will present at any given time.

- **narcissistic.** The narcissistic Bad Apple fears inferiority and needs to control situations in order to feel safe. They expect special treatment, demand your attention and try to recruit you to their camp, including isolating you from others in the workplace. They often talk about themselves, put down others and engage in one-upmanship. In their eyes, they are always right; others are always wrong!

- **sociopathic/psychopathic.** This type of Bad Apple is very rare. People with sociopathic or psychopathic tendencies tend to act in ways that are detached, unflinching and charismatic. They often demonstrate confidence, are very charming and can be clinically rational even under pressure. With a great ability to be focused, their notable lack of empathy means they have trouble making ethical decisions.

- **a woolly mammoth**. This person functioned perfectly adequately under the old system or previous manager, but they simply cannot make the transition to the new system or manager. They resent changes that they perceive to be unfair and disrespectful to the past. They take things incredibly personally, and often express an active dislike of the implementers of change.

When the team is 'toxic at the top', and the *manager* is the one behaving in harassing and bullying ways, the team is really in trouble. Good workplace culture must be clearly modelled and led from the top. If employees see upper management engaging in poor behaviour, this will undermine any good work done by Human Resources in promoting and enforcing good policies and promulgating the organisation's values. Some employees will see it as a licence to act inappropriately.

When a toxic personality is causing havoc at work, their colleagues won't want to become a target, yet they still need to achieve their own work goals and targets. It's difficult for managers to manage the Bad Apple, because Bad Apples are manipulative and sophisticated in how they conduct themselves. If confronted, Bad Apples are very good at avoiding responsibility, acting aggressively and diverting the blame onto others. They often make pre-emptive strikes, set people up and protect themselves—for example, by writing false and self-serving statements in emails so they can 'prove' their claims later.

A Bad Apple may be so difficult to deal with that no manager is brave enough to confront them. Some are passed from one team to another for years, creating problems wherever they go. As a result, they have no insight into their own behaviour.

When someone does finally try to hold them accountable, they respond aggressively—for example, by lodging a victimisation complaint.

IMPACT ON THE TEAM

A toxic personality in the team can leave everyone feeling on edge, resentful and drained. It affects team functioning, morale and cohesiveness. Table 3.1 outlines some common impacts on the team when a Bad Apple is rotting the whole barrel.

Table 3.1: common team impacts of a Bad Apple

Absenteeism	Toxic behaviour in the team can lead to sick leave and absenteeism, as colleagues opt out of the workplace to look after their own health.
Communication	The Bad Apple becomes the main person who speaks up in team meetings, with only one or two brave souls daring to raise alternative views.
Complaints	Some Bad Apples use internal complaints mechanisms maliciously to exert power over those who challenge their bad behaviour. They may lodge a formal complaint as a pre-emptive strike—for example, accusing their manager of bullying—when they foresee performance or conduct counselling on the horizon.
Co-opting	Certain colleagues believe the Bad Apple's conspiracy theories, not realising that they have been manipulated. They are then co-opted to fight the battles while the manipulating Bad Apple stays publicly silent.

Cooperation	People avoid working with the Bad Apple and minimise their interactions.
Factions	Factions develop in the team, pitting those who take the side of the Bad Apple against those who don't. The us-vs-them dynamic is often encouraged by the Bad Apple, as it suits their conspiracy theories.
Morale	Bad Apples can be incredibly influential on the team dynamic. Teams who have one member who is disagreeable are more likely to experience conflict, poor communication and lack of cooperation across the whole team.
Trust	Over time, people become increasingly aware of the Bad Apple's reputation for undermining others and nervous that they will become the next target.

If someone is behaving in negative, disruptive and undermining ways, the organisation has a responsibility to ensure that this behaviour does not cause harm to their colleagues. It also needs to contain the impact of that behaviour so efficiency and morale are not damaged.

For managers, supervising the Bad Apple is exhausting and nerve-racking. Responsible for managing the behaviours of a Bad Apple, as well as the fallout of their conduct, the manager seeks advice from HR and takes file notes of all interactions, in case they are later accused of bullying or unfair treatment. The Bad Apple sucks up 80 per cent of the manager's time, leaving other team members feeling neglected.

The team often doesn't know what the manager is doing behind the scenes to manage the Bad Apple, so the manager can appear to be ignoring the problem. This can damage the manager's authority and respect among the team.

Chapter 4

PERSONAL CRISIS
Someone is struggling

SYMPTOMS

- After taking a period of leave, a member of the team is often late for work with no explanation.

- Team members are unsure how to interact with their colleague, who is uncharacteristically moody and negative. They know something isn't right, but they respect the person's privacy. One person asks, 'Are you okay?', to be assured that everything is fine.

- Productivity may be affected as the team member is struggling to focus, make decisions and meet deadlines.

- The rest of the team feel frustrated and resentful that their colleague is not contributing at their usual capacity and that they are having to pick up the slack.

- The team member is spending significant time on personal phone calls at work, and appears distracted and at times distressed.

- Other staff members are drawn into extended conversations about the personal difficulties and welfare of their colleague and are negatively affected by these concerns.

If you or someone in your workplace is in crisis and you think immediate action is needed, call emergency services (000), contact your doctor or local mental health crisis service, or go to your local hospital emergency department.

To talk to someone for support in Australia, call:

Lifeline: 13 11 14

Suicide Call Back Service: 1300 659 467

beyondblue Support Service: 1300 224 636

WHAT'S GOING ON

People bring every aspect of themselves to work. This includes not only their skills and professional experience, but whatever is going on in their personal life, which might involve a divorce, a drug problem, a cancer scare, a gambling addiction or family troubles. We all have ups and downs, and sometimes people go through terrible challenges in their personal lives. This can make it very difficult for them to maintain a happy outlook and make a productive contribution at work.

Dealing with a personal crisis can seriously affect an employee's capacity to function as a productive, cooperative and contributing part of a team. If they are dealing with ill health or caring for a sick family member, they may require extensive time off or need to work more flexibly for a time. Usually, the workload and deadlines of the team cannot easily be adjusted to meet one person's lower capacity, so the absent employee's work is distributed among the remaining employees.

Often people dealing with grief, anxiety or depression find their productivity is affected. They may be distracted and unable to focus or concentrate, feeling stressed and emotional, and less able to handle the stress. They can find it hard to make decisions, manage multiple tasks or meet deadlines, and may also appear negative and less confident.

This may mean they fall behind and miss deadlines, or the quality of the work they are producing suffers. While in most cases this will be a temporary state of affairs, it can continue for an extended period of time and create tension for the individual and within the team.

The impact will be felt by other team members who have had to pick up the slack or deal with their team member's mistakes or unfinished work. You may find that other team members' patience wears thin as they become resentful or frustrated with their colleague's inability to contribute fully.

People struggling with a temporary personal crisis are *not* Bad Apples who need to adjust their conduct at work. They need our emotional support, as well as some well-placed, compassionate advice about how they are coming across to their colleagues.

Anxiety, depression and other mental health conditions

Everyone's mental health will vary throughout their lives. According to the Australian Bureau of Statistics' *National Survey of Mental Health and Wellbeing* in 2008, at any given time, three million Australians are living with depression or anxiety, and one in five employees are likely to be experiencing a mental health condition. If you look around you, chances are someone you work with is living with a mental health condition or has a family member who is.

Mental health organisation beyondblue explains that it is helpful to think of our mental health as being on a continuum, with good mental health at one end of the spectrum, and at the other end a variety of serious symptoms and conditions that can affect all facets of our lives. When someone has a mental health condition it can affect the way they think, act and feel, but it may have negligible impact on their ability to work. For some the impact is brief, for others it takes an extended period of time, or it may be an ongoing situation they have to manage. Everyone is different.

When people with a mental health condition have the right support and treatment, they can recover and lead healthy and fulfilling lives. Their supervisor and colleagues have important roles to play in assisting and supporting them in the workplace, and in educating and supporting the team of which they are a part.

Depression and anxiety are two of the most common and well-known mental health conditions. People with depression experience symptoms such as social withdrawal and difficulty in concentrating, and may feel guilty, unconfident and unhappy.

They have thoughts such as *I'm worthless* and *It's my fault*. They also experience physical symptoms such as feeling tired, sick and run-down, and sleep problems.

Anxiety is the continuing feeling of stress and worry, even after a stressful situation has passed. Feelings of anxiety may be ongoing and make it difficult to handle normal life.

Divorce, illness and other personal crises

The famous Holmes and Rahe Stress Scale lists life events that are correlated with stress and illness. It includes the death of a spouse or close family member, marital separation, personal injury or illness, and significant change in financial state. How many of these stressful life events have you experienced in the past 12 months? How many people in your team might have recently suffered from these events?

When people experience major negative life events, they have a variety of reactions. Expressions of grief, shame and fear tend to be stifled in the workplace as employees put on a brave face and do their best. Many who are facing difficult life experiences want to 'get back to work' to regain routine and a sense of normality, but they may not yet be 100 per cent ready. If the team knows what their colleague has been going through, the employee's personal crisis can become the elephant in the room. The employee tries (usually unsuccessfully) to leave their emotions at the door, and no one knows quite what to say to them.

In difficult times a person's effort to keep a boundary between their home and work life can be completely overwhelmed, because grief isn't easily disguised, and this can lead to further anxiety. Employees who have experienced a major negative life event may not talk about what they are experiencing but, like those suffering from anxiety and depression, they may display:

- an inability to concentrate
- lack of energy
- fatigue due to lack of sleep
- indecisiveness
- a short temper
- a range of emotions, including anger and intense sadness
- impaired performance and productivity.

IMPACT ON THE TEAM

People respond differently to others' trauma or emotional struggles. If a colleague is undergoing a personal crisis or managing a mental health issue, hopefully the team will respond with empathy and actively support them. Those closest to the individual may themselves feel sad or stressed as they attempt to support their friend.

There may, however, be other team members who are less confident—or less kind—in their responses. They may feel emotionally ill-equipped to support their colleague, or frightened about saying or doing something inappropriate.

There are many myths and falsehoods around mental health. Many people don't understand that a colleague who is managing a mental health condition can still function effectively at work. They may avoid interacting or working on projects with their colleague, which only serves to make the individual feel more isolated.

Unfortunately, there will be some people who are mainly focused on how their colleague's issues affect *them*. They may be concerned that their colleague's reduced work hours, absence or adjusted working arrangements will mean an additional workload for them. They may be uncooperative with managers' attempts to implement alternative working arrangements. They may even spread rumours about the situation. In the following case study, we see the full gamut of responses by team members, some helpful and some less so, when one of their colleagues is not functioning well.

CASE STUDY
GOING OFF THE RAILS

Recently John has appeared disoriented and grumpy in the morning. His personal hygiene is suffering, and he has started to get back to the office late after lunch. No one wants to say anything. It's all a bit awkward. Some of his colleagues at the courier company have a laugh behind his back. On two days the following week John doesn't come back from lunch at all. People suspect he is drinking at lunchtime.

John has always been very reliable and respected. Now his supervisor is worried about John's mistakes and slow execution, which seem to be becoming worse.

A couple of times, Sai-Wai overhears John shouting into the phone during his breaks. She is worried about him, as she considers him a friend. She has a quiet word with Rowan, who works in Human Resources. 'It's just not like him. He's not directing it at us, but he's obviously in a really bad place personally. He won't talk about it, but he seems to be going off the rails.'

One afternoon John has a minor accident in a company vehicle and returns a positive blood alcohol reading. In his subsequent discussion with Rowan, John explains that he is going through a divorce and is worried about his ability to see his kids in future.

Chapter 5

WORKPLACE ROMANCE
Keep it professional

SYMPTOMS

- Everyone knows that two members of the team are having an affair.

- One colleague is found crying in the bathroom or having long conversations on their mobile in the car park; often one or the other is absent from work altogether.

- Gossip is rife.

- The two colleagues now avoid each other religiously, refusing to engage with each other, even when they have to attend the same meetings or work together on a project.

- Team members are taking sides, or trying to avoid both of the former partners, causing ructions in the team.

- One or both employees are considering leaving the organisation.

WHAT'S GOING ON

Given the amount of time we all spend at work, it's not surprising that many of us will meet our romantic partner there. Although the percentage is decreasing (thanks to online dating), a significant number of us meet our partner at work. In 2015, around 10 per cent of American couples first met at work.

Note that in this section we focus on two colleagues who have been in a consensual romantic or sexual relationship that has ended—not one person inappropriately pursuing a colleague, which is called sexual harassment.

'Keep it professional'

Employees who are in a relationship at work often try to 'compartmentalise' their professional and personal lives, and hide their relationship from their colleagues. Usually this is not a problem until the relationship ends and strong negative emotions surface. The breakup of a relationship is bad enough without the added complication of having to see the former partners every day, undermining emotional wellbeing, job performance and professional identity, potentially damaging the dynamics of the team and even breaching company policies.

In breakup scenarios that play out in the workplace, a common challenge for those involved is how to hide their emotions—just as they have hidden their relationship from their colleagues—to protect their professional and personal reputations. They try to 'stay professional', as displays of emotion (particularly tears and obvious signs of distress) are generally frowned on.

Fallout from a breakup

A relationship breakup can also have a detrimental effect on work performance, whether or not the former partners work together directly. Both will usually have lower motivation and focus due to the grieving process, especially if their work places them in close proximity.

Partners sometimes misuse their positional power at work, either before or after the relationship has ended. This conflict of interest is a particular danger if one person in the relationship has the power to make decisions that involve benefits (pay, other rewards, leave applications, progression and training) or negative consequences (discipline, restructures, redundancies) which affect the other.

A further challenge for women involved in a workplace romance is the double standard by which men and women are sometimes judged. Women often fear being given negative labels such as 'seductress' or 'cougar' (if she is older than her former partner), or being accused of using sex to gain favour with men in the organisation. On the other hand, men may be forgiven or even praised: 'He's sowing his wild oats' . For this reason, women report that their professional identity and threats to professional reputation are significant issues when they break up with a partner at work.

Unwanted conduct of a sexual nature

An added risk for former partners is sexual harassment. Non-threatening 'pursuit behaviour'—such as repeated phone calls, text messages or emails, or other attempts to win the person back—might be considered 'acceptable' (if not agreeable) conduct between two former partners who do not work together. It is absolutely unacceptable in a work environment, as it can constitute sexual harassment or bullying. Former partners sometimes forget that their conduct towards their colleague is subject to employment policies, which apply a higher standard of conduct.

More dangerous is where one of the former partners deliberately harms the other—for example, by discussing intimate aspects of the relationship and breakup with colleagues, including lascivious sexual details. At its worst, the fallout can include:

- criticism and defamation of their former partner on a social media website

- deliberately undermining their reputation

- violent conduct at or after work and professional events

- disclosure to others of deeply personal, sensitive or embarrassing information about their former partner

- sexual harassment
- misuse of power in the workplace in retribution.

This behaviour can have very serious implications for employees' reputations, their relationships with co-workers, and the mutual respect and efficient functioning of the team, as well as legal risks. The following case study demonstrates what this downward trajectory can look like.

CASE STUDY
BATTLE AFTER THE BREAKUP

Angela and Ricardo were both married (to other people) when they started having a secret sexual relationship while working together at a travel business. After about eight months, Angela told Ricardo she didn't wish to continue the relationship. Despite this, recently Ricardo repeatedly asked Angela to have coffee with him, sent more than fifty emails to her personal email account, bought her gifts and left flowers on her desk. He also became unpredictable and was responsible for several emotional outbursts at work. Things became even more complicated when Ricardo's wife found out about the affair and contacted Angela's husband to tell him about it.

Ricardo's unwanted attention towards Angela continues. Angela has got to the point where she can no longer tolerate working with Ricardo and she lodges a complaint with Human Resources.

IMPACT ON THE TEAM

A workplace romance can undermine trust in the broader team. When there is an ongoing, consensual, sexual relationship between colleagues, there are sometimes perceptions of favouritism, exclusion of others and a breakdown of team relationships. Where one of the parties is more senior than the other, the other team members are often sensitive about fairness of decision making, such as access to training and other benefits.

After the breakup of a workplace romance, the damage can affect co-workers and be socially divisive in a workplace. Gossip and innuendo can thrive. Co-workers often 'take sides' and find it difficult to maintain a constructive professional and social relationship with both parties. The former partners can feel judged and become isolated, left out of social events and everyday conversations.

Occasionally, one of the former partners will choose to avoid the social aspect of work, because they don't want to hear news about their former partner or to have to fake feeling happy. In other situations, there is a risk that a valued employee will leave the organisation. This may lead to feelings of loss within the team or give rise to a sense of injustice that someone has been 'driven out'.

Another risk, both for the individual employees and for the organisation, is conflict of interest and the impression that decision making involving one or both partners was unfair. Fairness and the team members' *perceptions* of fairness are incredibly important to a trusting, harmonious and cooperative team. So is the team's perception of the integrity of the managers and decision makers. If there is any hint that the manager is not demonstrating integrity and making fair decisions based on the right criteria, that manager's credibility will be damaged.

When one former partner has the power to make decisions that affect the other, it is difficult for the less powerful of the two to believe that the decision was impartial and fair. One party often ends up assuming the worst of the other. This in turn can give rise to claims of discrimination, bias and even bullying.

We all know that a personal crisis can have an impact on work performance. After a breakup, the two employees' motivation and ability to concentrate might decrease for a period of time, affecting their performance. They are likely also to rely on their colleagues for support to achieve their targets and goals (hiding their temporary poor performance), as well as for emotional support. This can leave everyone feeling drained and resentful.

In the United States, it is now commonplace for employers to require employees to disclose any intimate relationships with colleagues. Written agreements known as 'love contracts' are signed by couples to acknowledge the rules within the workplace and protect employers from any potential fallout should the relationship sour. This level of intervention in office romance is not common in Australia, where the culture has traditionally been 'don't ask, don't tell', except in the policies on staff–student relationships in universities. This may change, however, following a number of recent high-profile cases involving workplace romances gone wrong.

Chapter 6

FAMILY TIES
The spectre of nepotism

SYMPTOMS

- Employees are married to each other, or to a colleague's sibling, child or parent.

- A close family member of a senior manager enjoys accelerated career progress. Other staff are silently fuming, seeing this as gross favouritism.

- Decisions about appointments and promotion are being made on the basis of who the candidate is related to, rather than their skills and experience.

- The 'favoured' family member becomes isolated and feels defensive, as the disapproval of colleagues seeps in. Alternatively, the favoured family member takes advantage of their power, knowing any reprimand is unlikely.

- The workplace is split into two camps: those who support the 'family-friendly' regime, believing such decisions to rest rightfully with the owners, and those who are outraged by a sense of injustice.

- There is a widespread perception that there is no point making a complaint about the favoured family member because they are a protected species.

WHAT'S GOING ON

Nepotism means the use of power or influence to secure unfair workplace advantage for members of one's own family. Where nepotism exists, the value under attack is *fairness*. An employee with a familial connection within the company will get ahead because of that connection, and not because they have special merit, skills or experience.

Many employers avoid recruitment companies and websites to minimise the cost and time involved in trawling through job applications and conducting numerous interviews, preferring to hire people whom they know. This is more common in small-to medium-sized family- and founder-owned companies. There is nothing inherently wrong with this—cost-saving is a valid operational goal—unless people are favoured for jobs and work opportunities because of who they know rather than because of their inherent merit, skills, experience, potential and values.

In any given recruitment process, as long as the practices are fair and have been applied without favour, no unfair favouritism has occurred, even if the member of an existing employee's family or friendship group gets the job. Sometimes, owing to remoteness of location or a limited talent pool, employers may have no other choice than to hire family members. In such cases, even where processes of recruitment and promotion have been scrupulously fair and objective, the *perception* of nepotism and its damaging effects can be hard to combat.

Employment of members of the same family can, under the right circumstances, be consistent with corporate good health. There are several important provisos, though.

Proviso 1

Be aware that where family members regularly apply for and get jobs in a company, there will be other staff who call it favouritism. No matter how scrupulously fair and transparent the recruitment processes are, such appointments are easy targets for disgruntled employees.

Proviso 2

Family members have trouble viewing each other with objectivity. For instance, a parent may be more forgiving of their daughter's failings than of someone unrelated who works with her. Family ties are stronger — and family rifts can be deeper — than relationships between unrelated work colleagues. This can add significant complexity to workplace issues, as we see in the following case study.

CASE STUDY
ALL IN THE FAMILY

Alexandra likes her job as a carer in an aged-care facility. When a vacancy arises at the site, she tells her brother Nick to apply for it. His application is successful, and for Alexandra work becomes more fun. She is increasingly happy and productive, as is her brother. Noticing this, the aged-care company adopts an official practice of paying a referral bonus to staff who encourage their friends and family to apply for jobs in the organisation.

Time passes and Alexandra is now the shift manager. Little family groupings are dotted across the company, and Alexandra believes this helps staff retention and cohesion. Over time, the demographic of the workforce is increasingly Greek and Samoan by family background.

As shift manager, Alexandra sets the roster each fortnight. Night shift and public holidays are less sought-after since the new industrial agreement came into force, as the weekend pay rates are less beneficial. Alexandra knows there's a family gathering planned on a Saturday two weeks from now, and she assigns those weekend shifts to staff who won't be attending.

Team member Samaria goes to see Alexandra to ask for a shift change, as she wants to travel out of town that weekend.

(continued)

**CASE STUDY
ALL IN THE FAMILY (*cont'd*)**

Alexandra turns her down, as she would otherwise have to assign the shift to her cousin or one of her best friends. Samaria feels that Alexandra discriminates against the Samoan staff. 'No favours for us', Samaria says in the lunchroom.

In this scenario, having opaque criteria for decision making will feed perceptions of unfairness. Even if Alexandra does make a fair decision, there will always be residual doubt about favouritism.

Proviso 3

The more power a person has in a workplace, the more caution they must exercise in recruiting or promoting a member of their family. Powerful people sometimes lose sight of the degree to which power disrupts decision making and lessens the likelihood that anyone will challenge them.

As we see in the following case study, honesty in performance feedback can be tested when an employee is related to a senior manager.

**CASE STUDY
THE NEW KID**

Ayuko and Bill work in the warehouse of a sugar mill. Jordan has recently joined the business. Ayuko says, 'That newbie is a useless little bludger.' Bill replies, 'Yeah, she's hopeless, but you were too when you first started! I could give her a few pointers.'

Sandro, the warehouse and packaging coordinator, comes along. Jordan sees Sandro and starts working very hard. Sandro

---

says to Ayuko and Bill, 'Gee, that new kid's impressive, isn't she?' Ayuko replies, 'Well, she's got a way to go yet. We'll see.' Bill says, 'We were just talking about how we could bring her on.' 'That's great,' says Sandro. 'I know you will be great mentors for her.'

Later that day, Ayuko and Bill learn that Jordan is in fact Sandro's niece. 'I can't believe Sandro has inflicted his useless niece on us', says Bill. 'It makes me so angry', Ayuko replies. 'I wish I could give my family jobs whenever they like. There are so few job opportunities around here.'

Sandro comes along later and asks, 'Has the kid had a good day? My sister says she barely slept last night, she was so excited.' Ayuko gives an insincere smile and replies, 'Great.' Bill says, 'We're making sure she feels welcome.' Sandro says, 'Thanks guys. It's important to the future of the business that she enjoys the work.'

In this scenario it's likely that work will continue with little visible disruption. Ayuko and Bill will probably, grudgingly, make sure the 'new kid' learns the job. However, a potentially corrosive discourse around favouritism and discrimination exists. Imagine if, at a later date, Jordan is given accelerated promotion. Whether or not the promotion is deserved, the resentment is likely to accelerate too.

Proviso 4

It bears mentioning that in some cultures nepotism is not seen as negative. Family support (including offering work opportunities) is a core part of loyalty and care for each other within the family group. Perceptions and understandings of equity and fairness can differ, so there may need to be an overt discussion about this in the workplace.

IMPACT ON THE TEAM

Where nepotism exists, non-relatives feel their skills, hard work and loyalty are devalued. They can feel excluded from opportunities they would otherwise expect to come their way. Those feelings of exclusion and wrongfully denied opportunities can become inflated. The effects of nepotism are insidious because they foster an escalation of resentments and a misinterpretation of favours bestowed and withheld in the work environment.

Over time, nepotism can cause other unintended consequences, including:

- erosion of staff engagement and ambition for advancement
- more staff leaving and declaring an intention to leave
- the possibility that the relative feels unaccountable for their performance and conduct at work or, conversely, that they must overachieve to prove themselves.

Conflict of interest

Nepotism constitutes a conflict of interest if decision makers favour their personal connections over the company's interest in having the best available person doing the job.

In practice, conflicts of interest can usually be managed through transparency and good governance. For instance, where a person responsible for assessing the tender submissions and awarding a cleaning contract finds that her nephew works for one of the tenderers, she can declare a conflict of interest and exclude herself from the decision. Such steps should publicly neutralise the potential conflict of interest.

Closed shop

Most worryingly, staff will feel that there is no point reporting to management any criticism of relatives of people holding power in the company. It is hard enough to report the perceived misbehaviours of *any* colleague: the disincentives always include a fear of repercussions. It is not hard to imagine how much worse repercussions might be if your report is about the boss's son, daughter or partner.

CASE STUDY
NO AVENUE OF COMPLAINT

Angela manages the research division of a major charity. She feels bullied by the manager of Operations, Albert, to whom she reports. Without articulating what he thinks is wrong with her performance, Albert recently required Angela to report to him weekly. All other managers report on a monthly basis. Albert also makes last-minute appointments with Angela that he then cancels or attends late. He has yelled at her about petty oversights, and his attitude of general criticism makes Angela very nervous.

She wants to report Albert's behaviour. The trouble is that the manager of Human Resources, the person to whom she could logically turn, is Justine, Albert's daughter. First appointed to a lowly position, Justine achieved a meteoric rise through the ranks to her present role leading HR. Angela's other avenue for complaint is directly to the chief executive officer, but the CEO's faith in Albert is well known. It was in fact the CEO who endorsed Justine as manager of Human Resources. 'It would be discrimination not to allow Justine to get ahead when she is such a fine candidate', the CEO announced at the time. Angela's strong sense is that Albert, Justine and the CEO would together shut down any complaint that Angela might make, even though her concerns are genuine.

Chapter 7

LACK OF DIVERSITY AND INCLUSION

The risks of a white bread workforce

SYMPTOMS

- Everyone looks the same, everyone has always looked the same … and everyone probably looks like the boss!

- They may not mean to be disrespectful, but team members are discouraging and offending customers, colleagues and stakeholders from other cultures. For example, they are impatient with customers who speak with a strong accent.

- If anyone in the workplace looks, sounds or thinks a bit differently, they don't get heard at all. As a result, they tend to keep to themselves, keeping their head down and making sure they don't give anyone a reason to target them.

- Capable staff who have different personal characteristics are not even considered for desirable work opportunities such as training and new projects.

- Because of how they are planned, social events that are supposedly for the whole team always seem to end up excluding some people. A couple of colleagues never attend.

- If a member of the team can't make themselves available outside work hours, they are seen as failing to contribute and as less valuable.

WHAT'S GOING ON

If a stranger were to walk into your workplace today, what would they notice about your team? There may be some notable, visible characteristics of the group to which you may not have really given that much thought. For example, are the team members all around the same age? What proportion of employees shares the same skin colour, cultural background, sexuality and gender? Does a certain type of person lead and succeed?

Having a team that is made up of the same type of people—mostly the same gender, age, ethnic background, religion and education—can go unnoticed. Homogeneity can fly under the radar when the composition of staff has not changed in decades, particularly in traditionally gendered sectors (nursing or mining, for example).

A lack of diversity can create risks to the team's functional abilities, culture and ethics. Employees can become victims of inequitable work practices when the people with power perceive them to be different, less worthy or more troublesome, as we'll see in the next case study. Typically, these groups have included: women (especially pregnant women, and women returning from maternity leave), people with carer responsibilities, ethnic minorities, people with disabilities, LGBTI individuals, employees who are active in unions (or non-unionised staff in highly unionised workplaces), people with English as a second language and some religious groups.

CASE STUDY
A ROUGH ROAD

Mark, the founding owner of a small construction business, recently employed Sally to run an all-male team of quantity surveyors, roadworks engineers and other building workers. Although Mark was somewhat wary of appointing a woman to

---

manage what he knew was 'a pretty blokey team', Sally was eminently qualified and had experience in a larger company.

Sally is keen to improve efficiencies, pointing out in meetings and on site inefficiencies in project design and rollout. Very quickly she meets resistance. A number of staff call her 'ma'am' in a mocking way, and refer to the company becoming a 'nanny-state' when Sally enforces health and safety procedures. Sally is accused of not understanding 'the way things are done around here'. Her attempts to challenge these opinions are met with silence. In her second month, she comes across a sign stuck up in the tearoom that reads, 'Ditch the witch'. Sally then overhears a colleague say, 'It must be the hormones', when she is rightly angry about a major error made by a worker.

Increasingly frustrated at being disrespected and stymied in doing her job, Sally telephones Mark. Mark does not return her call; instead he texts Sally that he has heard 'noise' about Sally's 'aggressive style', and maybe she needs to reflect about how she has been engaging with the staff. Sally is so angry at being treated as the problem, she takes a day of annual leave later that week to reflect and recharge. Upon hearing this, Mark texts her: 'Sally, sorry you found it too tough, and now can't do it due to stress. I will pay your entitlements. Happy to supply reference.'

Unfortunately, discrimination is not just something you read about in hypothetical case studies. It is all too common in Australian workplaces. The Australian Human Rights Commission reported in 2014 that higher levels of discrimination are experienced by people born in countries where English is not the main spoken language, people aged between 55 and 64 years, people with disabilities and Australian Muslims.

Obvious signs of discrimination are overt racism, sexism, homophobia and religious intolerance, such as:

- 'jokes' that are not funny to the victim
- graffiti on toilet doors and noticeboards
- hurtful 'pranks', which can involve physical violence
- refusing simple flexibilities that some employees need in order to practise their religion and that wouldn't affect their job performance (such as breaks at prayer time)
- ignoring religious festivals that some employees celebrate (such as Diwali, Eid and Hanukkah)
- operational decisions that exclude certain people (such as employees who are on maternity leave during a restructure process, or who cannot attend meetings after 5.30 pm).

Walking the talk

Ethical culture is led from the top. The board and the CEO may say they value diversity and equal opportunity, but are they walking the talk? Do decisions tend to encourage some types of people and discourage others? Are proactive reviews done of the demographics of new hires and promotions? No matter what the policies and procedures say, what are the employees (in particular, senior managers) actually *doing*? If the organisation's culture does not support working parents, people with carer's responsibilities, people transitioning to retirement, and people with religious and cultural commitments, for example, those people are being actively alienated.

We all have ideas, preferences, beliefs, prejudices and values that inform our decisions. Our views are shaped by our culture, upbringing, life experiences and many other factors. Unconscious bias—inadvertent, negative assumptions about the skills, aptitudes, behaviours or life choices of a person because of their personal attributes—will constitute illegal discrimination if it causes a detriment, or denies a benefit, to someone in the workplace. This is the case even if the decision maker is not deliberately causing a negative impact.

IMPACT ON THE TEAM

Discriminatory bias in the workplace has been illegal for decades in Australia. In addition to the legal, ethical, psychological and strategic risks, there are a host of missed opportunities for any team that is discriminatory or homogeneous, in terms of the employee value proposition, competition, innovation, customer service and stakeholder relations. Just as damaging to the organisation is the negative impact on the team's functional abilities, productivity, culture and output.

Groupthink vs innovation

Teams that are homogeneous in their demographic makeup tend to engage in groupthink, mulishly approaching strategic discussions, problems and key decisions in the same way. Often, in a homogeneous team:

- decision making lacks nuance and richness. Things tend to be done the way they have always been done, and the same things are always 'front of mind'.

- risks are miscalculated, competitive opportunities are missed and innovation is poor. The team lacks a variety of life experiences, information, political views, ways of thinking and observations of the outside environment.

- decisions go unchallenged.

Why is groupthink more likely in a homogeneous team? Two key reasons. First, if differences are discouraged, why would anyone speak up when they have a different perspective? Second, no one even realises there are better decisions that could be made. If all your employees share the same world-view and way of problem-solving, then the same mistakes will continually be made because of these blind spots. You may not even realise what you're missing!

When we interact with people similar to ourselves, we prepare less thoroughly, we fail to anticipate alternative viewpoints and we apply less effort in reaching consensus. Conversely, being around people who are different makes people more creative and better at solving complex, non-routine problems. Research by psychologists, sociologists, economists and other experts consistently shows that diverse teams are more innovative.

Productivity

A lack of diversity and inclusivity also damages productivity, as those individuals who do not fit the mould cannot bring the full benefit of their ideas and productive effort. Every time a Muslim employee who does not drink alcohol feels excluded from drinks with clients, a young employee is prevented from sharing her idea for a new product, or a transgender employee is overlooked for a secondment for fear they might not 'fit in', that employee's contribution is missed. The employee loses out, and so does the organisation.

Organisations often focus on technological advances to improve productivity, but what if we could enable 10 per cent of the team—those people whom we have inadvertently discouraged through discriminatory practices—to be 20 per cent more productive, simply by removing the impediments we have caused?

The moral hazard of sameness

A lack of diversity and inclusivity profoundly hurts the targeted and overlooked individuals. Employees who are seen as 'different' can feel isolated and disengaged. This can damage their productivity because they feel unsupported, they are offered less guidance and training, or they are excluded from social interactions. Exposure to direct discrimination has a significant negative impact on the individual employee's mental health, physical health, job attitudes, organisational behaviour and productivity. This has been proven in multiple research studies.

The ethical risks of allowing a 'white bread' workforce to continue unchallenged are pretty obvious. If the team thinks it is acceptable to discriminate against people, ideas, perspectives and approaches that are different, the organisation is condoning prejudice, allowing the team to act as if *achieving the best outcome* doesn't really matter. Quality of output, efficiency and merit are subjugated so the powers-that-be can maintain the status quo unchallenged.

Chapter 8

UNRESOLVED HISTORICAL ISSUE
Skeletons in the closet

SYMPTOMS

- Resentments between team members continue to stem from something that happened long ago, rather than a current issue.

- There's an 'elephant in the room' that the team doesn't feel it can openly acknowledge or discuss.

- Some employees are fixated on 'the way things were' before a past issue occurred.

- Employees are still highly emotional, which some colleagues and managers believe they should have got over. Those emotions might include grief, resentment, lack of trust in each other or lack of respect for management.

- Recent employees may not understand the reason for all this emotion if they weren't around when the past issue occurred. Those newer employees can't work out why their colleagues seem distracted and worried when the current environment seems safe and harmonious.

- There's a sense that certain issues are 'no-go areas' and shouldn't be discussed. The impression is that the organisation wants to pretend everything is okay, while some members of the team clearly think otherwise.

WHAT'S GOING ON

A skeleton in the closet is relatively easy to identify if you're aware of the recent history of the team. Simply put, there's an issue from the past (say, in the past two years) from which the team hasn't yet moved on.

Whatever the issue was, it was significant enough to rock the foundations of how the team worked together. It might have been:

- a serious complaint by one employee against another
- a critical incident or 'near miss', such as an occupational health and safety incident that harmed an employee or a client, which affected some or all of the team members
- the death of a loved employee or organisational founder
- the perception that an employee (past or current) broke the rules of the team in some way—for example, having an affair with a customer or engaging in fraud—that has damaged the whole team's reputation, even though others were not involved
- a decision by the manager that appeared harsh, and that the team cannot understand, such as terminating the employment of a member of the team in the week before Christmas
- a personal crisis that affected a team member and was ignored or poorly handled by the organisation (in reality or in the team's perception), such as denying the employee leave, denying a compensation claim or demoting them for poor performance.

The following case study highlights how a business-as-usual approach will not suffice when one member of the team has gone through a profound personal crisis and the future is uncertain.

CASE STUDY
A FAMILY TRAGEDY

Niro is a popular team member in the customer service division of a large electronics company. Most of the team have been with the company for a long time and they regularly socialise outside of work.

Niro's teenage son committed suicide last year. At the time, Niro took two weeks off work. Niro's manager, Felix, was concerned to protect Niro's privacy, so he did not disclose to the team what had happened and simply sent them an email stating that their colleague was 'taking some personal leave'. The team learned what had happened when one of them called Niro to see if he was okay. Many of the team members had met Niro's son and felt quite distraught. They tried to talk to Felix about what they could do to help Niro, but he closed down the conversation, saying it was 'Niro's private business'. When Niro returned to work a month later he suffered from regular panic attacks and took a break from dealing directly with customers.

A year later Niro has been taking extended periods of leave, and it appears he is struggling with depression, but this has not been acknowledged by Felix. It's not that Felix doesn't care, but he feels strongly that unless an employee comes to him and discloses a personal problem, it would be inappropriate to pry and raise it proactively, unless the issue is affecting their performance. Now Niro has been absent for nearly two months, and no one is saying anything about it. Niro's team feels sad and confused. No one knows whether Niro will come back to work, and the three people who reported to Niro are still reporting to a different manager 'on a temporary basis'. When they ask Felix about Niro's job, he just says, 'That's unclear.' Many of the team members are angry at the way Felix has dealt with things and think he should have done more to support Niro and his direct reports.

A key challenge, when a historic issue is still affecting the team, is the tension between *transparency* and *confidentiality*. Managers, Human Resources advisers and in-house legal counsel often know a lot about the historic issue, because they made a concerted effort to address it at the time. In our experience, the resolution of the issue is often kept private. Rather than being informed about what happened — who was disciplined, why someone was transferred to a different team, and so on — team members are left in the dark. Managers often err on the side of confidentiality and privacy, rather than sharing information with affected colleagues. Although well intentioned, this can seriously limit their ability to be open and transparent, and to encourage debriefing, healing and rebuilding within the team.

IMPACT ON THE TEAM

A skeleton in the closet can affect the team in numerous ways, not all of them immediately obvious.

Your team may be unable to work together productively because of unresolved issues between team members, or because an outstanding issue prevents them from moving forward. Employees may be cynical or jaded, questioning the motives of managers or making snide remarks about the way things are done.

The relationship between team members may also be affected when things that happened in the past have led to a lack of trust. For example, team members may feel angry or frustrated with an employee who they believe 'got away with' poor behaviour in the past or was treated with favouritism. This may lead them to isolate that individual, to be reluctant to work with them or to gossip about them.

Team members might also feel resentful towards senior managers they perceive as having managed the situation inadequately. They may believe the manager didn't truly understand the issues or the impact of the situation, or failed to give adequate consideration to employees' feelings. They may be cynical about management's capacity to effect change or do anything meaningful to resolve the situation. The manager may be viewed as hopeless or weak. In the following case study, we see the failure of an organisation to communicate about the resolution of a complaint and to restore professional relationships. It's a mistake that can affect workplace dynamics for years afterwards.

CASE STUDY
CLASHES CONTINUE AFTER COMPLAINT

Janice, who is manager of the university's international office, has a style that some of her colleagues describe as 'abrasive' and 'bossy'. Others believe she is unfairly judged because she is a woman in a senior position.

Eighteen months ago, Kah-Fai and Adele lodged a formal complaint of bullying against Janice. An investigation by an external consultant confirmed some of the allegations against Janice. She was found to have acted unreasonably by withholding information from colleagues, raised her voice on three occasions and twice failed to show respect to colleagues.

After the investigation of the complaints, which took some months owing to the absence of key staff, Janice was reassigned to a strategic project in the pro-vice-chancellor's office on a temporary basis, which she is disputing. The pro-vice-chancellor reassigned Janice for her own wellbeing, after she reported stress in relation to the 'vexatious and sexist' complaints. She was not disciplined in relation to the findings of the investigation. The PVC does not anticipate that Janice will return to the international office, although there is not an obvious, appropriate role for her after the strategic project is complete.

(continued)

> ## CASE STUDY
> ## CLASHES CONTINUE AFTER COMPLAINT (*cont'd*)
>
> Maggie has been acting manager of the international office for 11 months while Janice is absent. A new appointment to the manager role is expected once Janice's ongoing position has been clarified.
>
> The international office team was not made aware of the formal outcomes of the investigation, out of concern for privacy of the complainants, Kah-Fai and Adele, as well as for Janice herself. Staff have expressed nervousness about interacting with Janice while she is working on the strategic project. Kah-Fai and another team member have formally requested to know the investigation's outcome, but the PVC has stalled on making any decision on this.
>
> Donna, who is very vocal and an active union member, says she feels unsafe working with Janice and refuses to interact with her at all. Donna is assumed to be a spokesperson for the international office team, but other individuals have come to the HR manager confidentially with different views. No one really knows what happened to the complaint against Janice, why she was moved or whether she will return to manage the team. Kah-Fai and Adele's complaints against Janice appear to have been swept under the carpet, and to be something that can't be mentioned, even though many of the staff are still confused and hurt.

Loss of faith

Employees may have lost faith in the integrity of the organisation as a whole, particularly if they consider that what has happened is at odds with the values that the organisation espouses. For example, an employee is seriously injured because the company failed to comply with safety requirements, yet the company prides itself on embracing safety as one of its values.

Even if the organisation tried to deal with the issue in the past—for example, through disciplinary action and offers of counselling to employees—personal resentments, alliances and differing understandings of the incident can linger. Employees may feel disconnected with the organisation or with the managers, confused about the purpose of work, and ongoing grief for the loss of a loved colleague.

Get the full story

If you are the person charged with dealing with the skeleton in the closet, you may find it challenging to obtain the information you need to address the problem. Issues may be treated secretively or surrounded by mystique because team members don't know the full story. Perhaps they arrived after the events took place. Those who were around at the time when the problem arose may also be reluctant to discuss it because they are traumatised and don't want to revisit the past, or they feel guilty, or they have been directed not to talk about the event.

Your ability to find out what really happened and to communicate honestly and openly with your team will be integral to moving forward together.

Chapter 9

THE MANAGER'S STYLE
It's not the team, it's you!

SYMPTOMS

- All the employees in the team seem disengaged. They get the job done, but seem to put in minimal discretionary effort and do not offer ideas for how to improve systems or processes.

- The manager doesn't feel she is really connecting with the staff. It's a real effort to get them to agree to do anything outside their job description. Pushback is common.

- Turnover within the team is high.

- Team members regularly seek secondments and apply for roles elsewhere in the organisation. When applying, they do not ask the manager for a reference.

- Employees mostly seek guidance on work problems from one another rather than from their manager, whom they avoid.

- Employees appear guarded or nervous when giving the manager updates on how their work is progressing. Alternatively, they all appear to agree with the manager on absolutely everything. The worst feedback the manager receives from them is silence.

WHAT'S GOING ON

The stakes are high for leaders and managers. Every member of the team relies on them, at least to some extent, for guidance, direction, resources, feedback, approval and progression. We expect a lot of our managers, and when they fail to deliver, the backlash can be severe. Margaret Wheatley, the American adviser on leadership and ethics, suggests we expect our leaders to be 'heroes' who have all the answers. It's no wonder that leaders and managers feel under pressure to get it right.

And it's lonely at the top. Much information to which the manager is privy cannot be shared with the team for confidentiality and other business reasons. They have few peers within the organisation, and those they do have are often competitive and self-protective. Being in a senior position, the manager is unlikely to admit to feeling unprepared for the role or losing control of the way the team is functioning.

Sometimes managers and leaders lack emotional intelligence, or fail to see how they are really coming across. They are often doing their best, but they lack the nous, the trust of their team or the support of the organisation to hear and fully comprehend how they are performing in their management role. Some managers choose not to ask their team members for feedback on their decisions and management style, arguing that it would be 'unfair' to put staff in that position or that they would probably just say what the manager wanted to hear. Other managers try to get along with everyone, taking a laissez-faire approach. This results in the manager not really knowing what the team wants or what they might lack.

An important note: far less common—and even more destructive—are those senior people who apply manipulative, divisive and undermining tactics, in a misguided attempt to keep people on their toes and drive out those whom they perceive as weak. They apply a divide-and-conquer approach to create a power play and increase competitiveness. The expression 'the fish rots from the head' alludes to this kind of behaviour: the problems start at the top, and contaminate everything from there down. If the manager's problem is not their competence but their fundamental ethics, we point you to chapter 3, 'Toxic personalities', and chapter 2, 'Unprofessional conduct'.

At the other end of the spectrum, if the manager is under attack, check for upward bullying or undermining. Bullying—repeated unreasonable behaviour that causes risks to health or safety—can be directed at a manager by someone less senior (for example, a Bad Apple; see the 'Scoundrel or samaritan?' case study in chapter 13).

If the manager lacks skills, decisiveness or emotional acuity, it's important to remember we are all human. The behaviour of managers and leaders will be affected by the same factors as any other employee. These include the manager's:

- previous life experience and upbringing, including any conflicts or trauma
- childhood role models and influences
- personal values, desires and fears
- current and past workplace experiences
- anxiety over pressure from peers concerning their performance and the performance of their team.

These factors will consciously and unconsciously inform the manager's style, as we see in the following case study.

CASE STUDY
REPEATING HISTORY

Drazen is the clinical services manager at a national mental health service. During a 360-degree review, his team anonymously gave him feedback that his management style was autocratic and punitive. They reported that he micromanaged them and was unwilling to trust employees to manage projects, and that he was constantly critical of their work.

Drazen is shocked. He sees his management style as firm but fair. He thought he was helping his direct reports to learn by giving them honest feedback, but he now realises they do not experience his feedback in this way.

This evening he describes the feedback to his wife. She laughs and says kindly, 'The apple doesn't fall far from the tree, Drazen.' On reflection, Drazen realises that his management style was informed by his father's parenting style when he was growing up. His father had set extremely high standards and was constantly scathing of Drazen's attempts to meet them. He recalled the time when, at age 11, he got 97 per cent on a maths test, and his father had said, 'What happened to the other 3 per cent?' Drazen realises he is replicating that behaviour with his own employees.

In Drazen's case, anonymous feedback led to some affront and anger, but also to self-reflection and growth. It takes a combination of insight, commitment to self-development and targeted training to learn how to manage well.

Many of the leaders and managers whom we see behaving inappropriately or performing below par lack management experience or training. They may have risen through the ranks based on their technical skills and expertise in the subject matter—such as their sales performance or ability to write great audit reports—but they have had little or no management training. As management coach Marshall Goldsmith writes in his book *What Got You Here Won't Get You There* (2008), technical expertise by itself won't make you a skilled, trusted and ethical leader.

The five most common problematic management styles we see are these.

- **Avoidant:** You avoid challenging conversations, giving feedback or bad news, and making difficult decisions. You don't hold team members accountable for their performance or their conduct. Perhaps you wish to be friends with your team, saying 'yes' all the time; perhaps you doubt your ability to judge when to be strict. You avoid anything that feels like conflict.

- **Command and control**: You micromanage your employees and your area of accountability. You discourage input and feedback. It's your way or the highway. Employees who speak up, offer new ideas or fail to meet your standards are judged harshly.

- **Unpredictable:** Emotionally changeable, you frequently lash out emotionally at your employees. You act aggressively when stressed and do not tolerate signs of weakness in others.

- **Old-school**: Your worldview is not in line with your organisation's values. You speak and act in discriminatory ways. You discourage modern notions such as flexible work and diversity initiatives.

- **Political player**: You 'manage up' and are obsessed with ensuring you are seen to be an excellent achiever, regardless of the impact of unreasonable deadlines and overwork on your team.

In the following case study we see how a manager can fail to hold others accountable if they are disengaged, determined to be liked and to avoid conflict.

CASE STUDY
ACTING UP ON THE ASSEMBLY LINE

Night shift manager Peter has been at the manufacturing company Acme Industries for eight years now. It's pretty cruisy for him, as the team seems to be going fine. Although there has been a bit of pushback towards management, the team meets its targets much of the time.

Peter is keeping his eye out for alternative roles, as there isn't much chance of progressing at Acme and he's a bit bored.

The crew mostly keep to themselves. On a few nights they have taken long breaks, and all seven left the site on break at the same time, which they are not technically supposed to do. Peter asked Edo about it once, but then he felt a bit silly for raising it with the blokes. After all, everyone knows the night shift can have a rotten effect on your family life and it's important to be flexible.

One night they get back at 1 am and are pretty trashed. Peter says to Iosefa, 'Come on mate, don't you think you've had one too many?' but Iosefa just laughs and heads back to the plant. 'Just give it a while before you drive the forklift', Peter calls after him, laughing somewhat nervously.

The next day, Peter checks the swipe card records and finds they indicate falsely that only two staff left together, which means they are swiping each other in and out to cheat the shift rules for work hours. Peter could say something, but he wants to be one of the boys.

IMPACT ON THE TEAM

When leaders or managers are unreasonably aggressive, laissez-faire or incompetent, this has an immediate and direct effect on the team members. Employees want managers who are firm but fair, whom they can look up to and trust to lead them. Without good management, the team can become jaded, frustrated and disengaged, and will increasingly lose faith and confidence in the organisation. Productivity, morale and energy can all suffer.

If the manager is applying a 1960s-era management style and is ego-driven or micromanaging, some employees may see this as a licence to behave poorly themselves. For example, a manager who is disparaging of clients or talks over the top of his team in meetings is sending a message that respecting others is not a priority.

When employees experience disrespectful, offensive or humiliating behaviour from their manager, some become anxious, depressed or angry. Employees will be loath to confront the manager—or even more, to make a complaint to HR—but at the same time they wish the manager would learn and earn their respect. Other employees will become increasingly detached and silent. They'll work to rule and have no unnecessary involvement or interaction with the manager. Instead, they'll look for work elsewhere or seek an internal transfer.

Whatever problematic management style the manager is applying—avoidant, command and control, unpredictable, old-school or political player—they will have little ability to manage performance constructively. Clumsy attempts at giving feedback (if attempted at all!) can trigger a negative loop. As the individual employees' confidence suffers further, their motivation and discretionary effort spiral down.

In the worst-case scenario, the manager may be on the receiving end of a formal workplace complaint, a claim for workplace injury or illness, or even legal action. Not only costly and time-consuming for the organisation, formal complaints can affect the manager's own reputation and career progression.

Chapter 10

UNHEALTHY COMPETITION
Winners and losers

SYMPTOMS

- If you asked the team members what their mantra is, they would likely say, 'Win at all costs.'

- The team members do not collaborate with or contribute to one another's work. They are reluctant to share clients or leads, and they fiercely guard market intelligence.

- Employees have been known to undermine one another, even at the expense of the team's achievement of its goals.

- Long work hours are very common.

- They seek out specific projects with recognisable 'wins'—projects they believe will get them ahead of their peers—but they are reluctant to volunteer for any other work.

- Team members fawn over the manager, constantly praising their boss's skills and approach (no one is that good!). They ingratiate themselves with whomever they perceive to have power in the organisation.

- In private conversations with the manager, employees criticise colleagues' work performance when it is barely relevant.

WHAT'S GOING ON

Healthy competition can be a great motivator, inspiring people to perform at their best, energising them, increasing productivity and creativity, and multiplying the successes of the whole team. Competition that is cooperative sees employees working together to achieve, making the team greater than the sum of its parts.

At its most extreme, however, competition can actually do the opposite. It can give rise to a 'dog eat dog' mentality where employees will go to extreme lengths to outdo one another. Unhealthy competition pits employee against employee, creating stress and defensiveness. Aggressive employees will climb over the top of their colleagues to get ahead, leaving frustration, insult and damage in their wake. They take risks that the organisation does not sanction, and take advantage of any loophole or vulnerability. They will win at any cost, exploiting customers, breaching values and breaking laws.

The underlying assumption in such a fiercely competitive environment is that there must be a winner and a loser. This psychology centres strongly on the individual, and runs counter to the idea that collaboration and teamwork are the best ways to achieve the organisation's goals. The belief is that a team of hotshots will all try to outdo each other, ratcheting up everyone's output … and if one or two people bomb out, they didn't cut it, so their departure shouldn't be mourned. This type of competition fosters backstabbing and undermining, leading employees to waste time watching their backs and protecting their turf.

In many workplaces, competition is an intrinsic part of the culture. It can therefore be very difficult to strike a balance between encouraging your team to compete in healthy ways to perform at their peak and creating an individualistic culture that militates against team success.

If the symptoms referred to above sound familiar, you need to look at what is driving the anti-collegiate behaviour you are observing.

Ask yourself: What kind of team culture is my organisation promoting?

Start by examining what conduct and outcomes are explicitly rewarded and encouraged in your team. For most organisations, Key Performance Indicators (KPIs) are part and parcel of goal-setting, supporting strategic plans for the organisation, and ensuring employees are accountable for their time and output. Your organisation may have KPIs that prioritise what is achieved—for example, '270 widgets are built each week'. Having purely quantitative KPIs—whether volume of sales, dollars earned, number of new clients, patients seen or any other numerical standard—will drive your employees to focus solely on achieving this output.

Problems can arise when this is the sole criterion for how employees view success. If you do not also include in KPIs *how* the quantitative goals are achieved—*How do we treat each other on the widget assembly line? How much damage does our operation do to the environment? How much legal risk are we prepared to take?* and so on—then you are sending a message that the 'how' is not important. From the perspective of the team, how they achieve the quantitative KPI is left to their own devices. What is to stop them cutting corners, taking health and safety risks, ignoring longer-term goals or alienating stakeholders, in order to reach the KPI?

It won't matter if your organisational policies or values set the parameters of appropriate behaviour. If the message to employees is that you only value 'what' they achieve, and that 'how' they do so is secondary, the organisation could inadvertently set up a culture where the ends justify the means. A driven and competitive team that has only quantitative outcomes as KPIs will drive individual behaviours that are self-centred, uncollegiate and suspicious.

Within workplaces, internal competition can derail collaboration and trust. If team members are competing with one another in a dog-eat-dog culture, fear prevails.

This type of culture can be exacerbated when the one or two 'rainmaker' employees (who bring in the highest sales, investment income or other quantitative achievement) are untouchable. If the rainmaker employees are allowed to get away with anything, and are not held accountable for their bad behaviour in the workplace, this sends a clear message to the rest of the team: 'Achieve this KPI using whatever means necessary, and you will be rewarded.' Beyond your team, consider whether this might be happening at other levels of the organisation. Is excessive competition occurring between teams to the detriment of the company culture as a whole? What outputs and behaviours do the CEO and other senior executives visibly promote and reward? What messages are they sending? Does the organisation value collaboration, respect, collegiality and trust, or solely the number of widgets (or equivalent) that are produced or sold? Unbridled competition and a laissez-faire culture can lead to a complete breakdown of accountability, as we see in the following case study.

CASE STUDY
COMMISSION AT ANY COST

Jeff and Yee-Fui are sales agents in a city-based commercial real estate agency. Jeff is charismatic and well-connected; he uses his charm to build relationships. Yee-Fui speaks Mandarin fluently and focuses on the overseas investor market, which is lucrative.

Every member of the sales team is paid almost completely on commission. If they make no sales, the agents earn very little income. This means the team competes ferociously. Each agent maintains a separate marketing database that they guard secretively, and they do not share the leads they are supposed to share in team meetings. They are more focused on beating each other than building the business.

With loose management and a 'flexible' approach to compliance, breaches start to creep in. Jeff convinces the sales director to falsify a document, which leads the compliance officer to leave the business out of fear for his own personal liability. Meanwhile Jeff accuses Yee-Fui of 'stealing' two buyers, who telephoned the agency to speak with Jeff but then struck up a conversation in Mandarin with Yee-Fui. Arguments ensue about who is entitled to what percentage of the commission on some big sales.

Factions form, broadly along ethnic lines. The agency's market share starts to trend in the wrong direction. Meanwhile staff accuse each other of cut-throat conduct and not being 'on the same page', but no one takes individual responsibility for changing their own behaviour.

Other drivers of a destructively competitive culture are:

- limited pathways for career progression, pitting individual employees against their peers
- grading all employees' performance on a curve — no matter how well they perform as individuals on an objective basis, unless they 'beat' their colleagues they will be ranked down
- industries, such as banking and sales, that are highly profit-driven and competitive, and in which the main vision and mission are easily described in quantitative terms

- a high proportion of the team thrives on stress and perform optimally in high-stakes environments
- a weak or ineffective manager (chapter 9) allows bad behaviour to go unchecked (chapter 2), which serves to confirm that the end output is the only thing that matters.

IMPACT ON THE TEAM

A culture of unhealthy competition can have an increasingly corrosive effect on values, legal compliance, discretionary effort for non-KPI activities, communication, mental health and morale.

It's quite possible that employees are working hard and producing what they have been asked to produce. Judged on the singular criterion of *volume of output*, the team may be exceeding expectations! This is not sustainable over time, however, because while the team works with that goal as their only yardstick, they are creating unnecessary risks (in particular, reputational and legal) for the organisation, focusing on short-term goals at the expense of longer-term goals, and undermining one another's wellbeing. The quality and sustainability of output will ultimately deteriorate.

Striving for advantage in a culture of unhealthy competition, employees will often find workarounds for rules and regulations they perceive to be slowing them down or limiting their output. In our experience, they commonly avoid seeking the approvals required for planned actions, underestimate the size of a contract spend in order to avoid the delays of procurement processes, work around compliance measures, overcharge clients (for example, lawyers 'inflating' their timesheets) and apply predatory sales tactics in order to win more work from customers. Staff can also apply pressure to external and internal legal advisers, as well as risk and compliance officers, to sign off on things that involve significant risks to the company, just to meet their own KPIs.

Unhealthy competition can also drive overwork (chapter 12), and has an uneven impact on those who have interests and obligations outside work, including family commitments (chapter 7).

Chapter 11

NO CLARITY,
NO ACCOUNTABILITY
The path to
Complete Chaos

SYMPTOMS

- The team's critical work is usually completed, but at the very last minute and often with undue stress. Other tasks are forgotten altogether.

- Some members of the team seem to be permanently underutilised or are busy with tasks that don't contribute to achievement of the team's goals.

- Plans change halfway through projects, and deadlines are often extended out of necessity.

- Some colleagues are trying to implement improvements, while others happily remain responsible to no one and accountable for nothing. Manipulative or malicious employees exploit the confusion to their own ends, creating power plays and undermining the manager.

- There is growing cynicism towards particular managers.

WHAT'S GOING ON

From an outsider's point of view, teams that operate in chaos may not appear to be dysfunctional. Some teams with no clarity of structure, KPIs, accountabilities or reporting lines can simply muddle along, seemingly on cruise control. These teams often do achieve an acceptable level of output. After all, the bar has been set quite low for them. The problem is they won't have time or inclination for tasks that are important but less urgent, or for value adding, for example through innovation. They are achieving far less than they could if they were operating efficiently and with clarity of focus.

The primary symptoms of Complete Chaos are *inefficiency* and *confusion*. Deadlines are missed or pushed back. No one is quite sure who is responsible for restocking the stationery cupboard, chairing the team meeting, inducting the new employee or signing off on project stages. Meetings are confused and slow, their purpose unknown, the agenda vague and outcomes unclear. The same issues are discussed repeatedly, but there never seems to be any progress.

Pinpointing the cause of the chaos in such teams is not complex, because you are conducting a check of *what is missing*.

No clear reporting lines

Teams operating in chaos are often hamstrung by vague and duplicated reporting lines: the organisational chart contains dotted lines, indicating multiple supervisors. One person reporting to two or more people creates a blurriness of accountability, as well as inefficiencies in manager–subordinate catch-ups. This can allow people who don't wish to be held accountable for either their performance or their conduct in the workplace to avoid accountability altogether.

Similar challenges can exist if the manager works remotely, or some of the time in different offices, unless both the manager and the direct reports are diligent with remote communication and follow-up.

No role clarity or individual goals

Poorly defined roles have been recognised by workplace safety regulators as a significant stressor for employees. Every employee in the team should know exactly what is expected of them, by when and to what standard. Ideally, they should also understand how their individual efforts fit in with the team's efforts and the organisation's pursuit of its goals. Failure to provide this clarity will lead to uncertainty, stress, tension and conflict between colleagues.

It is inevitable that employees' roles will change somewhat over time, as a result of:

- the employee's experience and skill development
- the employee being promoted or transferring to a new position or project
- the arrival of a new supervisor or manager
- the restructure of a work unit
- other things going on in the team and in the organisation.

The problem is not the change itself; it is failure to adjust the role expectations to match the change. Unless the supervisor ensures that the employee is clear about what the change means for their work, the employee may feel unsafe, disengaged and undervalued.

No accountability

Lack of accountability is another thing that can lead to Complete Chaos. In this situation, the manager and team members expect very little of each other. The good performers will keep on delivering—they are wired that way. Lazy, incompetent, ill-fitting and under-resourced employees will keep failing, because no one is calling them on their mistakes or engaging with them to find out what can be done to help them achieve.

Often it feels too difficult to call out a colleague on their broken promises and fudged commitments. Perhaps it feels risky or like a source of conflict that could be avoided. Sometimes it just seems easier to do the task ourselves. This is true only in the short term. By failing to hold others accountable for their performance in the team, *we become part of the problem*, and all we can expect is more disappointment, frustration and resentment. Without accountability, the weak performer will keep missing deadlines, showing up late, playing on their phone in meetings, cutting corners and breaching their commitments. Without accountability, the quality and integrity of the whole team are chipped away.

Insufficient managerial skills or supervisory effort

Does the team have a 'reluctant' manager? You know the type—the manager who's not really a 'people person', who has checked out of the role, who fails to explain her decisions properly, or who prefers to stay in her office with the door closed. Perhaps the manager lacks communication skills. Perhaps there are things going on in the team (or affecting the team) that he doesn't have the skills and power to handle. Maybe the manager himself is overworked and overwhelmed, so the best he can do is hope the team is okay and put out spot fires when they appear.

Sometimes the cause of Complete Chaos is the supervisor's unwillingness to make decisions about priorities, so the team knows what to focus on and what *not* to focus on. This can allow a culture of chaos or overwork to develop.

Whatever the reason, the manager who fails to provide proper direction and oversight lets the team down on a fundamental level.

In the following case study we see elements of all four causes of Complete Chaos: no clear reporting lines, no role clarity or individual goals, no accountability, and insufficient managerial skills or supervisory effort.

CASE STUDY
ANARCHY IN THE ARCHITECTURE FIRM

Grace is a project manager at a medium-sized commercial construction firm. Over the years, her job has encompassed everything from training new recruits to coordinating major development projects. Grace loves her job and has been an asset of the firm for nearly a decade.

Recently the firm has grown significantly, and the sophistication of the safety program hasn't quite kept up. The firm's founding owner decides to bring on a new senior health, safety and environment officer, Oliver, whose responsibilities will include managing the safety aspects of three new major projects on the east coast. Oliver will manage the safety officers on every project, ensure compliance with policies and support the site teams.

In the past, Grace had oversight of safety at her own projects, with the safety officer reporting directly to her. The owner's view is that the HSE regulations are so strict, and the firm's safety culture needs such a shift, that a dedicated senior HSE manager is required. The owner decides that Oliver's role will report to him, but with a dotted line to Grace. The first Grace hears of this is via a firm-wide email announcing Oliver's impending arrival at the firm at the end of the week.

Oliver immediately approaches Grace to get up to speed on the east coast project. Upset that she wasn't consulted about Oliver's hiring, and aware that Oliver half-reports to the owner, Grace

(continued)

CASE STUDY
ANARCHY IN THE ARCHITECTURE FIRM (*cont'd*)

asks one of the team to show him around the site. Grace doesn't invest any further time.

Over the next few weeks, Grace ignores Oliver's request for guidance on some operational matters. Oliver is struggling to work out the processes for getting things done, as most of the procedures are in Grace's head, and he is working remotely every second week. The owner asks Grace how Oliver is going, as his dotted-line report, and Grace emails back, 'He seems to be doing okay, but you'll be across all his substantive work.' Meanwhile, a near-miss occurs on the east coast site, and Grace blames Oliver. Oliver is outraged, as he has received only pushback from Grace while working to change the culture around incident prevention.

IMPACT ON THE TEAM

The impact of chaos can be felt at both team and individual level. The symptoms described above have obvious effects on the productivity of the team as a whole. Not all employees are working to an optimum level and there is an uneven distribution of work. Goals are unclear, as are the means by which the team is supposed to achieve them. It's not surprising that this negatively affects the team's culture, motivation and relationships. It also increases the potential for work-related stress and overwork for certain team members.

At an individual level, in the free-for-all that is a chaotic team, team members don't feel that their level of personal effort or achievement is being noticed or checked by anyone.

In a team suffering from Complete Chaos, *conscientious colleagues* will work harder to pick up the slack. They fill the management void by proactively suggesting improvements that will keep the team engaged and achieving. However, those strong and previously dependable performers will eventually get tired of carrying the load. They will grow resentful of others (both the ineffective leaders and the slack team members) who are not pulling their weight.

Meanwhile, Complete Chaos can be a haven for *under-performers*. Because responsibilities and standards are not clearly articulated, communicated or enforced, the under-performer can remain inadequate. Indolent and incompetent employees can kick back and put their feet up—sometimes literally—while they mess around on social media, chat in the lunchroom or watch as their colleagues complete team tasks.

Teams in Complete Chaos often demonstrate incredibly uneven performance across their members and carry a 'dead weight' staff member who achieves almost nothing. No one knows what they do—whether or not they appear to be trying—or why the team's manager tolerates this person's complete failure to contribute.

Also taking advantage of the confusion are any *manipulative or malicious* members of the team. A lack of clear order for the way the team should be working creates a vacuum. This vacuum will be exploited by the Gossip, the Unprofessional team member and the Toxic Personality (chapters 1, 2 and 3). The mischievous employee delights in the combination of a weak manager, a lack of accountability and a lack of clarity about what everyone is supposed to be doing. This is the perfect opportunity for them to create havoc, undermine the manager and play off one colleague against another.

All of this means that respect between team members dwindles, and the manager has an increasingly tough time guiding and motivating them. Cynicism and frustration are rife, and the manager feels out of control.

Chapter 12

OVERWORK
Team stretching, presenteeism and the 24/7 paradigm

SYMPTOMS

- The team is incredibly busy, all the time. Everyone is highly productive but highly stressed. People feel overloaded and depressed by their inability to keep up with the work demands.

- The employees appear to be constantly physically exhausted, burned out and drained of energy. People seem to get sick often, and when they do, they work from home rather than taking sick leave to recover.

- Errors are creeping into the work outputs. People are too exhausted to pick up typographical mistakes at 11 pm. They accidentally delete files, miss emails and double-book meetings. Important deliverables are sent out without being finessed or checked, because deadlines can't be met comfortably.

- Team members become annoyed over trivial things, such as the photocopier malfunctioning. They are testy and irritable with each other.

- Shared activities—such as cleaning the office kitchen or celebrating birthdays—fall by the wayside. Bigger picture conversations, like strategic planning, similarly do not happen.

- There is less spontaneous daily engagement and socialisation. The team's focus is entirely on work, work and more work!

WHAT'S GOING ON

That last symptom gives it away, doesn't it? Work, work and more work.

According to the Australian Bureau of Statistics, in 2016 the majority (4.6 million) of Australia's 7.3 million full-time workers worked more than 40 hours per week. Of that group, 1.4 million worked more than 50 hours per week, and 196 000 more than 70 hours per week! Given that legislation prevents Australian employers from requesting a full-time employee to work more than 38 hours in a week unless the additional hours are 'reasonable', a significant proportion of us are overworking.

We have all had times in our lives when our job was stimulating and we were developing our skills. Then we might not have minded working some extra hours to get ahead and build our careers. Throw in some outside interests, family commitments or personal challenges, however, and long working hours are not so doable.

Every team has peaks and troughs in workload to meet fluctuating demands. It becomes a problem when the whole team is under heavy strain for a sustained period of time, and there is no sign of the workload lessening.

Overwork and the consequent risk of employee burnout can be more likely when any of the following factors are at play.

Downsizing

Over the past decade, downsizing has been a common phenomenon across many sectors, often following a restructure, the arrival of a new executive or a corporate merger.

Unless careful decisions are made, reducing head count can result in the fewer remaining employees in the team being under immense pressure to complete the same workload.

Team stretching

Over time, some employees leave the organisation altogether, or take extended leave (for maternity, carer's responsibilities, long service, illness, study or secondment). Although there is no official process of downsizing, the failure to backfill or replace such employees has the same effect. Remaining employees are expected to stretch their capacity to complete additional tasks or deal with unforeseen circumstances, initially on a short-term basis. If the organisation is slow to fill employee gaps or ignores them altogether, the reduced team's increased workload becomes 'the new normal'.

Presenteeism (long hours)

In some workplaces, consistently working long hours (whether or not they are productive) is seen as evidence of the employee's loyalty, contribution and commitment. This can mean that employees stay at work late into the night, mainly in order to be seen to be doing so. Some even leave their jacket on the chair and the computer on, so it looks like they are still at work but temporarily elsewhere in the office! Employees feel pressure to show up at work even if they are sick or underutilised; physically present, they are not necessarily productive.

The irony of such a culture is that working long hours does not actually result in greater output. Recent Swedish research suggests that productivity actually increases when employees are working a *shorter*, six-hour day. In addition, rewarding long working hours rather than the quantity and quality of work output has a discriminatory effect on those who need to leave the office for personal reasons.

A workplace that drives its staff to work long hours can be particularly damaging for those employees who have a tendency to overwork, because of their ego, fear of failure or wish to avoid a stressful situation in their personal life.

The 24/7 paradigm

We are all increasingly connected throughout the day and night, anywhere in the world, through technology. Smartphones and tablets, as well as video-call applications, enable fully connected remote working for some jobs. There are many positive outcomes, particularly enabling flexibility in how we work, and with increasingly globalised work across time zones. But the flipside is that, along with the four walls of the office, the clear divide between work time and leisure time has evaporated in some industries. Work calls or emails regularly occur at unsociable hours, yet many organisations do not track and recompense employees for additional time worked.

Overtime

Much of the overwork we are talking about is unpaid overtime. Research conducted by the Australia Institute in 2014 found that Australians together contribute $110 billion worth of unpaid overtime to employers each year, with full-time workers contributing an average of six hours a week overtime, and part-time workers an average of three hours.

Unpaid overtime includes staying back late, working through breaks, taking work home and answering emails out of hours. The situation is also problematic for those working part-time, particularly if they are juggling parenting or carer's duties at the same time: one study found that 52 per cent of part-timers were found to experience role overload.

A culture of overwork can take a toll on employees' performance and wellbeing, as we see in the following case study.

CASE STUDY
DENNIS THE MENACE

Xanthe is a law graduate at one of the largest law firms in the country. Dennis, the high-profile litigation partner for whom Xanthe works, is renowned for eating breakfast at his desk after pulling all-nighters when working on a big court case. Xanthe has worked 15-hour days in the past week, sorting through evidence with lawyer Vigo. Vigo is recovering from chronic fatigue syndrome and under doctor's orders to limit his work hours.

The Friday deadline looms ever closer. Dinner is provided in the boardroom every night for those who are working on. As the week wears on, Xanthe is becoming increasingly tired and stressed. On Wednesday night she sleeps in the sick bay, as she'd rather get an extra two hours' sleep than commute home at midnight.

Keen to maintain her reputation in the cut-throat firm—where lawyers judged by the partners to be inadequate performers are frozen out—Xanthe feels she can't say anything about overwork, because Vigo's health comes first. When she asks Dennis if she can leave at 5.15 pm on Thursday, he tells her 'the deadline is the deadline' and 'I'll be around at 7 am on Friday morning to keep an eye on you, don't worry'. One of the other lawyers overhears their conversation and tells Xanthe that during her first year she needs to do 'whatever it takes' and suggests she dose up on caffeine.

On Friday morning, Xanthe has a shocking headache and feels close to tears. She realises she has missed an entire box of documents, but she is too anxious to tell Dennis that they are not going to meet the 4 pm deadline.

IMPACT ON THE TEAM

If left unchecked, overwork can lead to serious risks—risk to psychological and physical health, and to productivity, as well as legal and reputational risks—for your organisation, your team members and you.

The long-term health impacts on team members are significant where high workloads continue. Working more than 55 hours per week is associated with an increase in risk of incident coronary heart disease and stroke, as well as diabetes and depression.

Overwork has ramifications for employees' personal lives as well. They may struggle to unwind and feel too tired to exercise to rejuvenate. The demands on team members working regularly into the evenings and across the weekend may cause frustration and dissatisfaction, and eventually burnout, departure or illness.

When employees' private time is overtaken by work, unpleasant and unanticipated consequences flow, including:

- poorer health and more stress
- increased levels of absenteeism due to physical, mental or emotional fatigue, and a decreased commitment to the job and organisation
- more use of prescription medications
- more dissatisfaction with their close personal relationships
- employees choosing to have smaller families or delaying starting a family
- negative impacts on employees' perception of the organisation and their sense of pride and connection to where they work.

Overwork and stress can also have an impact on *how* the work is done, with employees cutting corners to get the work finished, avoiding compliance with processes that they perceive to hold up completion, being less consultative and collegiate in how they work, and being less creative and innovative.

In overworked teams, employees keep their heads down and take little time for breaks. This limits the time they have to engage with one another or enjoy day-to-day social niceties, such as greeting one another each morning, having coffee together, developing workplace friendships or those incidental human interactions that make the workplace a more pleasant place to be.

Clearly, the real costs of overwork far outweigh any false perceptions of increased output—in all organisations except those whose explicit plan is to use up and burn out staff within three or four years for commercial reasons, with no regard for their wellbeing.

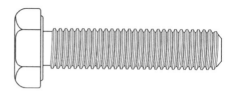

PART II
THE FIX YOUR TEAM TOOLKIT

While reading Part I of this book, you've probably experienced a few lightbulb moments. Do you have a new insight now into the dynamics, personalities, behaviours and drivers that are messing with the functioning of your team? Having reviewed the 12 common team problems, some will have jumped out at you—the familiarity of some of the scenarios we've just reviewed might even be shocking.

To recap, the most common problems that cause havoc to a team's functioning, morale and productivity are:

Gossip culture

Unprofessional conduct

Toxic personalities

Personal crises

Workplace romances

Family ties

Lack of diversity and inclusion

Unresolved historical issues

The manager's style

Unhealthy competition

No clarity or accountability

Overwork

At this point in *Fix Your Team*, you will likely have identified more than one challenge that needs to be addressed, and none of them will be simple. Separate problems or overlapping issues may be evident. This means that you may be feeling overwhelmed, having identified so many problems that you don't know where to start.

Do not fear! In Part II, first we will ask you some practical questions that get to the heart of the complex and thorny issues that are hindering the cohesion, values and functionality of your team. We will then set out the Fix Your Team Toolkit: the six Fixes that dysfunctional teams need, and the Tools you can apply to achieve them. They are as follows:

The Fix: Address unhealthy conflict

Tool #1: Train everyone to have important conversations

Tool #2: Offer facilitated discussion, mediation or conflict coaching

The Fix: Address unconstructive individual behaviour

Tool #3: Counsel the Bad Apple or unprofessional team member

Tool #4: Get the organisation to investigate the apparent misconduct and discipline the wrongdoer

The Fix: Develop the team's character and connections
Tool #5: Next hire
Tool #6: Develop self-reflection in the whole team
Tool #7: Build the team's connections

The Fix: Align with values
Tool #8: Diversity and inclusion initiatives
Tool #9: Make sure the organisation's values and behavioural expectations are known, clear, understood and real
Tool #10: Build a culture of feedback

The Fix: Develop leadership and management
Tool #11: Train the manager
Tool #12: Ensure clarity — hold people accountable!

The Fix: Care for each other
Tool #13: Support the team through personal crises and challenges
Tool #14: Dealing with overwork

For quick reference, a summary of the Fix Your Team Toolkit can be found on page 247.

Finally, to give your Tools the best chance of success, Part III guides you through the key elements of designing and executing your plan: a plan that will bring you—and the rest of your team—peace of mind, renewed focus, improved connection and refreshed enthusiasm for your workplace.

Chapter 13

WHERE TO START

People and relationships are complex. Emotional intelligence is needed to identify and address such issues. These skills are often referred to in business literature as 'soft skills', which misrepresents how incredibly difficult it can be to get a group of human beings to work together constructively for years! This isn't the easy stuff. It requires the manager to be a multi-skilled combination of psychologist, motivational speaker, police officer, visionary, ethics adviser, management consultant, subject-matter expert and more. It also requires members of the team to be emotionally intelligent, flexible, savvy, politically astute, forgiving and constructive!

Now, let's work through some practical questions that get to the heart of the complex and thorny issues that are pulling your team off track. In these reflective exercises we will take a broad view of the context, culture, history and future horizon. These perspectives will deepen your understanding of the team dynamic, and also of how amenable the team will be to different interventions. A workbook of these reflective exercises can be downloaded at www.fix-your-team.com.

INDIVIDUAL DYNAMICS, CONTEXT AND CULTURE

First, *think about the individual people* in your team — about their behaviours, personalities, styles, preferences and personal circumstances. Are they acting in ways that are aggressive, fearful, confused? Are they avoiding responsibility for their work outputs or their conduct? Do they spend quality time together? Are they absenting themselves from work (legitimately or otherwise)? Do they help each other, achieve goals together or compete in ways that are destructive to morale? Consider their motives and what might be driving them.

Reflect on the *interpersonal dynamics* between members of the team, and between team members and the manager. Are they constructive, engaged and respectful? Avoidant, dismissive or combative? Are there silos and factions within the team, or between the team and other groups in the organisation?

Now consider the *organisational context*. What changes, unusual events or systemic issues has your team lived through? Have restructures had an impact on them? Have the organisation's operational decisions translated into more work for them, new expectations in their output or work methods, or less job security? Are changes in the industry causing a sense of uncertainty around the future of their jobs? What are they facing in the near future? Are there threats or opportunities on the horizon?

Next, think about the *external context*: the political, economic, social and competitive environment. These elements are likely out of your control, but they may well affect the team's experience. What influence could systemic factors be having on your team dynamic? Consider:

- **the sector/industry.** Is the sector or industry growing or in decline? What are some of the major challenges it currently faces? How do they affect the work your team does?

- **the regulatory framework.** Have there been any recent legislative changes that are affecting the work your team performs? Does the current regulatory framework cause unwanted changes or enable innovation?

- **the stakeholders.** What influence do external and internal stakeholders have on your team? For example, is your workload performed predominantly for a few key clients who wield a strong influence over how things are done?

When people are facing change and uncertainty at work, some feel anxious, vulnerable and unbalanced. Others feel invigorated, liberated and brave. These responses can cause people to act in ways that are defensive, withdrawn and blaming, or conversely in ways that are strategic, cooperative and focused. Change can bring out the worst and the best in people. It disrupts and tests the ways the team used to work.

Next, how would you describe the *culture of the team*? Workplace culture is made up of the shared values, assumptions, beliefs, symbols and behaviours, implicit and explicit, that exist in a team. Culture guides how choices are made in an organisation, and the ways that people approach their work. When thinking about your workplace culture, consider:

- what it feels like to work in this part of the organisation

- how team members interact with each other, in formal and informal settings

- what you see and experience every time you arrive at work (the vibe of the place)

- the values at the heart of the organisation's operational decisions

- the organisation's decisions about its people: how it engages, manages, rewards and disciplines.

We're thinking now about the actual culture that employees experience, not the culture that the company is striving to achieve. The set of values that the organisation *says it subscribes to* may be realistic or aspirational, fanciful or nothing more than a public relations exercise.

Use the following words as a prompt to think about the culture of the *organisation as a whole* and the values that drive it. You will probably think of other descriptive words too. Circle those that apply (or add your own) below. *Be honest!* Choose the words that really describe the organisation as it is functioning now.

accountable	empathetic	interesting
adaptable	empowering	kind
agile	engaged	learning
anxious	equitable	mean
blaming	ethical	mindful
caring	exciting	overwhelming
challenging	excluding	performance-
changing	expertise	driven
collaborative	fair	professional
collegiate	family-	purposeful
competitive	friendly	quirky
controlling	fearful	respectful
courageous	flexible	responsible
creative	focused	ruthless
critical	fun	sad
curious	growing	siloed
customer-	guarded	strategic
centred	hectic	supportive
cut-throat	hierarchical	teamwork
depressed	honest	traditional
dispirited	inclusive	transparent
distrusting	individualistic	trusting
diverse	innovative	unethical
divided	integrity	unforgiving
dynamic	intense	

Now review the full list again, this time considering the culture of *your own team*. Are there any differences? How distinct is your team's culture from that of the organisation as a whole? What do you think has created that disparity?

While thinking about culture, there are several points to keep in mind.

Firstly, there are subcultures within all organisations. Organisations that are highly functional can contain dysfunctional teams, and vice versa. The possibility of dysfunction is heightened when the team is geographically or functionally separate from the rest of the organisation, when the team's manager has a strong and distinctive style, or when the type of work the team does is very different from the work of the rest of the organisation (such as the risk-averse finance division of a boundary-pushing creative agency). Some parts of the organisation may have a healthy subculture where staff are aligned in following the values, while elsewhere the values are either missing in action or honoured mainly in the breach.

Remember, too, that each member of the team will have their own experience of what it feels like to be an employee of that organisation. An organisation that one employee finds competitive, performance-driven and fun, another employee might find cut-throat, individualistic and excluding.

If you have an extremely divided team, try the exercise above from the perspective of two very different team members. What would each of those two colleagues say about the team's character?

For every characteristic, goal or value that the organisation has, there will be other things that are valued less. For example, if the organisation is guarded and traditional, it is less likely to be innovative and to allow employees to get things wrong. Which characteristic is the organisation privileging over other potential options?

Finally, even admirable traits can become dangerous if taken to extremes. For example, a company's focus on profit and competitiveness, without a concurrent focus on being family-friendly and safe, could drive a culture in which compliance and wellbeing suffer.

Next, review the 'symptoms' of the 12 different dysfunctions examined in Part I. Having thought through the behaviours and conduct of your individual team members, the recent history and the cultural context in which they are working together, which of the symptoms are familiar to you? Which ring true for your team? Create a shortlist of the dysfunctions that might exist in your team. It may be that some of the dysfunctions seem familiar but you can't quite put your finger on the problem just yet. Don't worry if the dysfunctions are not completely clear to you at this stage. Just take a note of some of the possibilities.

IS THE 'SURFACE' PROBLEM HIDING THE REAL PROBLEM?

Be aware that the most obvious explanation for underperformance, poor conduct, conflict, disruption or obstruction may not in fact be the true cause. Sometimes the apparent problem is in fact a distraction from the real issue. Keep an open mind, as the truth of the situation may become apparent only after some exploration and fact-finding, as we see in the following case study.

CASE STUDY
SCOUNDREL OR SAMARITAN?

Senior manager Hala is concerned about gossip among the direct reports of manager Armand, who was found to have acted inappropriately about a year ago. Now there are rumours that Armand is 'touchy-feely', acts in a superior way to the clients of the nonprofit social service (parking his Alfa Romeo outside a community centre), and takes his laissez-faire approach to management so far that he is rarely seen in the workplace.

Hala calls in an external workplace consultant. The consultant knows that the reality of situations is often quite different from

---

individual perceptions of them. She speaks to all the employees, some of whom request anonymity in their meetings. Employee interviews reveal that, in fact, Armand is the target of a campaign of discrediting and undermining by two toxic team members. Those two employees slander Armand, whose Alfa Romeo is borrowed from a friend while his own old Honda is being repaired, whose previous warning for 'inappropriate touching' was confined to putting his hand on a colleague's shoulder, and whose absences from the workplace are all explained by increased visits to clients, which he had been instructed to make in his last performance development meeting.

As a result, the two rabble-rousers are counselled and reminded of the organisation's expectations around professionalism and respect. Armand is given coaching to help him actively manage difficult employees, be more present and build better connections with the whole team.

IS MORE THAN ONE PROBLEM AT PLAY?

At the heart of the dysfunction in your team might be an *individual problem* (a toxic personality, a poor manager, someone being allowed to behave badly ...), a *big picture problem* (culture, unclear structure or roles, unhealthy competition ...) or a *mix of problems*.

Many of the team dysfunctions we outline in this book also *create other problems* for the team, leaving behind a very messy situation indeed. Here are some examples:

- A laissez-faire manager puts the management of a Bad Apple in the 'too hard basket' and ignores it. This damages the team members' trust in, and respect for, the manager.

- A workplace romance created issues that are still unresolved (skeleton in the closet), which fuels a gossip culture. Employees are talking among themselves about lascivious details of one another's personal lives.

- Complete Chaos lets a toxic personality run riot. Toxic personalities are very good at seeing opportunities they can manipulate to their advantage, and exploiting gaps in accountability and visibility.

- When unhealthy competition is incentivised, this can lead to a culture of overwork, with people attending the office for extra hours, and answering emails at all hours of the night and on weekends. This can have a particular impact on team members who have carer's responsibilities, which can in turn damage the team's inclusive culture and diversity.

If the challenges your team is facing are complex and multilayered, don't worry. The tools in the Fix Your Team Toolkit can be applied separately or together, as part of the same project or in sequence. The tools can be implemented with a small group of employees, the whole team or even the whole organisation! They all improve trust, harmony, cooperation and accountability in the team.

So long as you have identified the dysfunctions that your team is experiencing—no matter how messy, historical or hard fought—the following chapters will guide you to identify the tools that will make a positive difference.

DO YOU NEED MORE INFORMATION?

It's possible that, while you suspect you know what's going on in the team, you have a strong sense that there is something hidden—something under the surface that you can't quite identify. It may be that you need more information before you can confidently diagnose the problem. There are some good ways for you to obtain more information about the team's experience of the dysfunction, its symptoms and side effects, to help you to decide the path forward to Fix Your Team.

Whatever your level of confidence about what is going on, consider these methods of gathering more data.

1. Get more data about the team's perspective on the dysfunction

Often, members of the team will be grateful for the opportunity to talk to someone well-meaning about what is going on, if they are given an opportunity to do so. It is incredible how revealing and helpful these discussions can be, and how perceptive employees are about what they are experiencing and what the organisation could do to improve things.

The key conditions for their honesty and openness are:

- the **opportunity to participate**, without being forced to do so—allow employees to control who hears their views

- **trust** in the person who is gathering, analysing and reporting on the information—if there is a lack of trust in their direct manager, who may be perceived to have vested interests in certain outcomes, a colleague from another team or division might assist

- the option of **anonymity** for team members if they wish to minimise their fear of repercussions and victimisation.

How do you go about obtaining the views of your team members in a way that is carefully managed, has integrity and is trusted?

Ask the team

Unless the team is so broken that employees can't have a safe and open conversation at all, the starting point should always be an internal, informal attempt at resolution *before* you resort to external options. Ideally, this will be conducted by the manager of the team. The manager can, either on their own initiative or with prompting, hold a meeting to discuss the dysfunction openly.

Yes, this needs to be handled carefully, so it doesn't appear to be (or descend into) blaming either by the manager or by the team members. The manager should model a curious and open-minded approach, trying to understand the issues from the team's perspective, and avoid jumping too soon into identifying a solution. Instead of presenting their version of the problem, the manager could open a discussion by making an observation and asking questions.

'Team, I've become concerned recently about how we are communicating with each other in stressful times. Has anyone else had concerns?'

...

'I've noticed that people seem to be relying on email instead of talking in person. Is that right? Is there a reason for that, do you think?'

...

'It's important to me that we receive input, ideas and feedback from everyone. Do you feel comfortable speaking up in team meetings? How are you finding the channels of communication these days?'

...

'Recently I noticed the CEO refer to the organisational values in her monthly email. Are the values familiar to you? Do they provide practical guidance for how we as a team treat each other and pursue our goals?'

...

'I've recently noticed that people seem reticent about sharing information and reluctant to work together on projects. Would you agree with that? What do you think is driving that?'

...

'Is there anything going on within the team that I should know about?'

Everyone will learn something from the discussion that follows.

Workplace review

A workplace review is initiated by the employer to uncover what the employees think is going on in the organisation, or a department or team, and what they think needs to be done to improve the workplace. Typically, the review will be conducted by an independent consultant (rather than HR, which might not be perceived as impartial), who gathers information from employees, makes an objective assessment of the situation, and offers feedback and recommendations to the organisation.

The consultant asks broad, open-ended questions that encourage the employee to talk, such as 'How do you feel about coming to work each day?' and 'If there were three things you could change about this workplace, what would they be?' The information that employees share in workplace reviews is incredibly useful to the employer. Perhaps surprisingly, employees are usually very candid, thorough and direct in the information they volunteer. People like to feel heard!

After all the data has been collected, the consultant draws out the themes, concerns and opportunities the employees have raised and reports back to the employer, with recommendations for future improvements. Here's an example of how a workplace review can unearth the factors that are dragging the team down and inform the plan for a new future.

CASE STUDY
INTERVIEW INSIGHTS

Super Employment Group, a recruitment business, has experienced a huge turnover in employees and has received some negative feedback via exit interviews. Those employees who have stayed appear to be feeling unmotivated and disengaged. New HR manager Aaron decides to get to the bottom of the problem.

Aaron invites every member of staff to a confidential one-on-one interview. Through the interviews, Aaron comes to understand that a previous manager (who had since resigned) had created discord and friction in the team through his abrasive management style, including playing off one employee against another, which created silos. Many team members are contractors who work remotely, and felt disconnected and isolated. Now the manager has left, employees are relieved but still feeling rattled and unconfident.

Armed with this feedback, Aaron and the new manager, Philippa, are able to put in place a number of strategies to develop the relationship between the new manager and the team, and to rebuild trust and collaboration. Starting with an offsite meeting, Philippa informs the team of what the workplace review had identified, and seeks their input and support to create new ways of working. She celebrates the hard work of those who stayed on, and makes a commitment to the team that the working culture will change.

The team decides to conduct a structured weekly meeting, which includes those who work from home, using Skype. Philippa also works with Aaron to identify opportunities for different team members to work together on key accounts, so they get to know each other better and are rewarded for collaborating.

Twelve months on, the team is cooperating and performing well, and the level of trust is returning.

Importantly, organisations should only implement a workplace review if they intend to inform the employees (at least in general terms) about what the review has found and what the organisation will do about it, as Philippa and Aaron did in the case study. If you ask your employees for their input on how to improve the workplace, then you appear to do nothing with it, the employees will become even more jaded and cynical.

Employee surveys

An annual employee engagement survey or more frequent 'pulse check' can achieve different objectives from a workplace review. Employee engagement surveys commonly explore themes such as:

- employees' understanding of the organisation's mission, vision and values, and the extent to which employees relate to them

- whether responsibilities and performance standards are clear and achievable

- how challenging, engaging and rewarding the work is

- the diversity of teams, the effectiveness of anti-discrimination initiatives and the cultural competence of staff

- the extent to which employees have the resources and support they need to do their job
- the career path and development opportunities that are available to employees
- whether leaders and managers behave ethically, take action and create a vision for employees to believe in.

Surveys can be tailored to the organisation's particular areas of interest, or sourced 'off the shelf' from online providers such as SurveyMonkey (www.surveymonkey.com).

An annual survey usually asks the same questions every year, to enable benchmarking or tracking results over time, and is comprised mostly of ratings on a scale to enable quick analysis of large amounts of data. These characteristics limit the survey's ability to achieve a deep dive into particular issues. For this reason, many organisations are moving away from annual surveys, and using more flexible and frequent pulse checks. These shorter surveys, also conducted online if that medium reaches all staff, allow the organisation to explore employee opinions about specific initiatives, proposed reforms and aspects of culture.

By contrast, workplace reviews gather far more detail, and are a concrete demonstration of the employer's interest in what each employee has to say. As a collaborative process, it invites participants to contribute to the development of creative solutions. This can help generate engagement and loyalty in staff, build a sense of ownership and influence over how they work, and also encourage a workplace culture of reflection and autonomy in improving how things are done.

2. Gather data from Human Resources or online databases

In many organisations, Human Resources holds vast amounts of people-related data, such as performance ratings, demographics, skills, experience, tenure, safety record, educational background, managers, prior roles, progression, and leave and attendance records. In larger organisations with good information systems, this data is held in databases that senior staff can access directly. This rich source of information may give you a better feel for what is going on in your team, if you are in a position to access it. The quality of the data available and the ability to mine that data will depend on the size of your organisation, the resources available, and privacy or confidentiality requirements.

Even if you work in a small organisation, you may be able to analyse basic information to derive some insights: Does your team have a higher-than-average turnover, when compared across the organisation? What do people say in exit interviews? If employee surveys have been completed recently, how does this team compare with others in the organisation in terms of their reported engagement, satisfaction, trust in their manager and other relevant factors?

Think about what the data is telling you. Are there any notable trends? Does anything surprise you? Does any of this information confirm, or contradict, your preliminary thoughts about what is going wrong in this team?

3. Managers: Learn more about how you are perceived

If you are a manager or leader of a dysfunctional team, and chapter 9 resonated with you in any way, congratulations. Congratulations for being self-aware and brave enough to admit that there might be something about the way you are managing this team that could be improved.

If we truly believe that everyone can and should develop professionally over the course of their career, and that it's always possible to do things better and learn from our experiences, we should apply those same beliefs to ourselves. A good manager should always be open to receiving feedback, as well as giving it. There are various ways to learn more about how you are perceived in the workplace and identify how you might do better in your management of the team.

- **Ask for feedback in real time**. At the end of a meeting or discussion, ask someone how they felt the interaction went and how you could do better next time. You could also appoint someone as the meeting commences to observe and provide feedback to the whole team.

- **Ask a member of the team**. Only try this if there is someone in the team who you *genuinely believe* will feel able to be honest with you about how you are perceived. If such a person exists, ask them to give you direct feedback. You could explain that you are doing some self-reflection and professional development (after all, you are reading this book!), and that you'd like to gain further insight into your management style—what is working and what isn't, and what you could do to improve. Do not attempt this with someone who might be intimidated by the conversation, or who you think will give you only positive feedback. Remember, you want 'warts and all' feedback, from someone who'll tell it like it is and not just give you polite affirmation.

- **Ask a peer to review you**. Ask a peer who has good visibility of your work to review your performance and give you honest and objective feedback about how you operate.

- **Set up a 360-degree review**. A 360-degree review is a tool by which an employee can obtain feedback from a range of employees about their performance. The employees who give feedback will be team members, more senior managers, peers and subordinates—hence the '360 degrees'. The feedback is usually provided by four to eight other employees.

- **Get an external perspective**. Talking with a coach, mentor or counsellor can be a great way to get an independent and fresh perspective on your management style, improve your decision-making and interpersonal skills, and elicit guidance on challenging issues. Make sure you work with someone who is experienced, and who is honest with you about what may be happening in the team, your own contribution to it and how you could do better. Someone who is a friend of yours may not be able to do this for fear of hurting your feelings.

It's important to keep in mind that the more you ask for feedback personally (by whatever means), the more you earn permission to give feedback to others, and the more you support a culture where feedback—including discussing risks and applying an innovation mindset—is the norm for everyone.

It can be difficult to hear feedback from people who report to you, particularly if it is negative. In her book *Mindset* (2006), Carol Dweck, a Stanford University psychologist, maintains that your mindset will play a large part in how you respond to feedback. She distinguishes between people with a *fixed mindset*, who believe their intelligence and talent are fixed traits, and those with a *growth mindset*, who believe their basic abilities can be enhanced and improved through dedication and hard work. A person with a growth mindset will see constructive feedback not as disapproval or criticism, but as an opportunity to learn how they can further improve and enhance their skills and performance.

Once you have received feedback about the areas of management in which you can improve, take the time to digest it, possibly away from the workplace. Keep an open mind about the feedback you receive. Just because someone disagrees with your approach, it doesn't mean you have to change, but all feedback should be seen as an opportunity for development. We'll return to this in chapter 18.

WHAT IF THE WHOLE ORGANISATION IS BROKEN?

When a corporate scandal breaks, it almost never involves only one lone wolf who has been acting against the regulations and values of the organisation—no matter how much the organisation might want to claim so. In our experience, there is usually a *culture* that incentivised, allowed and rewarded employees, directly or indirectly, for behaving in corrupt and inappropriate ways.

Think of some of the corporate scandals in the media recently: banking staff who were encouraged to evade tax and launder money overseas, high-profile men who have engaged in sexual harassment and child abuse for years, misogynist initiation rituals in the military, conspiracy to mislead regulators over environmental emissions regulations, repeated frauds by government ministers. Would any of this wrongdoing have been possible on such a long-term and significant scale, had the culture of the organisation—as understood by every individual involved—not allowed it?

Sometimes the team is broken because the whole organisation has been hit by massive, external events. The entire organisation may be:

- exhausted from rounds of restructures and retrenchments—a common example is government departments that experience regular overhaul for political reasons

- experiencing massive change, for example in an industry where technology is making the key products obsolete

- recovering from a major scandal that led to the resignation or termination of the board or the

CEO, the shame of all the staff and damage to the share price

- so large, broken and immovable that any attempt to address the toxicity—which spreads across many teams—feels pointless
- dealing with a major shift in its culture due to a merger with a very different organisation.

Such significant challenges have a direct impact on teams across the whole organisation. Each team will respond according to its own subculture, values, strengths and weaknesses; however, your team is not completely at the mercy of these events. It is not impossible to fix a broken team even if the rest of the organisation has challenges of its own.

The challenge for teams in such situations is to work out what they can influence. There will be a reality that the team cannot alter—such as a new board, competitive headwinds or poor corporate reputation—but the way we treat each other every day, in our own team, is within our control. We can choose our own attitude (Tool #6), address our own conflict (Tool #2), protect one another's wellbeing by addressing overwork (Tool #14), upskill the manager to care for team members who are struggling (Tool #11), and more! At Worklogic we have seen many teams that know their purpose, work cooperatively, support one another and achieve remarkable things, even when those around them are giving up.

Change fatigue, fear of retrenchment, obsolescence—these are awful things to face in your team and in your career. But happiness is determined more by the attitude you as an individual bring to the situation than by the forces that buffet you. Team culture is chosen by the team, not determined solely by the wider organisation. Even in the wildest of circumstances, you can Fix Your Team.

THERE IS NO MAGIC BULLET

A sense of urgency and a strong desire to act are common at this point. Remember that human dynamics are complex and cannot be resolved with a quick fix. Before you decide on the interventions that will Fix Your Team, keep in mind that this will likely be a medium-term turnaround. Most teams will need a month or two to achieve a significant shift in their behaviours, attitudes and culture, and some will need even longer. There's no fail-safe remedy for issues that stem from people's behaviour and culture, however. There is no magic bullet!

Often, when a manager decides on a management intervention, there is a tendency for them to feel that they have already done their job and the issue has been addressed. Don't assume that your decision to apply a tool or delegate its execution (to a colleague or an external consultant) is all that is necessary. Keep a medium- to long-term view. Track progress. Be aware of possible derailers, and be ready to adapt or change the tool if the team responds in unexpected ways.

Keep in mind what success will look like, and the value of what you are working to achieve. Remind yourself that this work can be messy and complex, but the gains for the whole team—in productivity, quality of working life and health outcomes for your colleagues—will be worth it.

CHOOSING THE INTERVENTIONS

By now you should have built a picture of the problems that you and your team are facing. Following the steps set out so far in this book, you will have:

- reviewed the *symptoms and characteristics* of the 12 dysfunctions that could be disrupting your team
- considered the *individual people* in your team, how they are behaving, their motives and what might be driving them

- thought through *recent events* that your team has lived through, any *potential change* on the horizon, and the likely impact of these on team members

- described the *culture of the organisation* that the team is working within

- gathered any *further information* you need to understand the problem better, possibly including feedback and ideas from the team members themselves, employment data and self-reflection assisted by a coach or mentor.

At this point, give some thought to the end goal that you want to achieve for the team. *What, fundamentally, needs to change for this team to get back on track?* This will guide you in choosing what Tools you need to apply. The Fix Your Team Tools examined in the chapters that follow are organised to achieve the unique Fix that your team needs.

Ready?

Let's Fix Your Team.

Chapter 14
THE FIX
ADDRESS UNHEALTHY CONFLICT

CREATE UNDERSTANDING AND RESTORE TRUST AND COHESIVENESS

The Tools in this section include facilitated discussion within the team about the dysfunction, the more formal methodologies of mediation and conflict coaching, and training everyone to have important conversations. If your aim is to resolve conflict in your team, build understanding, and restore trust and cohesiveness in how team members work together, start here.

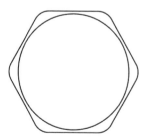
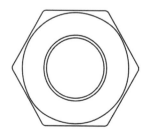

Chapter 14

THE FIX
ADDRESS UNHEALTHY CONFLICT

CREATE UNDERSTANDING AND RESTORE
TRUST AND COLLEAGUES

TOOL #1
TRAIN EVERYONE TO HAVE IMPORTANT CONVERSATIONS

It's natural to feel nervous or even dread about having conversations on important issues with our colleagues. Many of us will go out of our way to avoid them! Speaking with a colleague about issues such as performance concerns, a complaint against them, inappropriate behaviour, organisational change or redundancy can be confronting and challenging.

There's an art to having these conversations, and it's worth learning by everyone in the team. Equipping your employees with these skills will give them confidence, reduce stress and engender a culture of tackling difficult issues in a measured and timely way. Of course, these are skills that are relevant in other areas of life—your family and friends will be beneficiaries too.

Failure to conduct these conversations well, or even to have them at all, can be incredibly damaging to the team. It allows the following dysfunctions to persist:

- **Nasty conduct in the workplace**. Avoiding tackling this issue sends the message that different rules apply to certain people, and that the organisation lacks integrity (chapters 1, 2 and 3).

- **Unresolved issues from the past**. If these aren't dealt with, the team suffers grief, frustration, factionalism and/or resentment (chapter 8).

- **Weak management.** The manager cannot set standards and hold people accountable unless the important conversations are identified and held (chapter 9).

- **Poor performance**. The poor performer does not realise that the standard of their work is low or how they can improve it, usually due to the absence of strong management (chapter 9).

- **Confusion over roles, reporting and accountabilities**. This can lead to Complete Chaos (chapter 11).

Everyone in the team needs to be able to identify unspeakable issues, and to have the courage and skill to give feedback in a way that is future-focused and constructive. Here are a few key principles for having important conversations.

1. Be proactive

If there was something lacking in your own performance, you would want to know about it so you had the opportunity to improve, right? The reality is that almost everyone wants to know if there is a problem with their own performance, yet almost no one feels comfortable giving negative feedback to a colleague, even if it's part of their job as a manager.

If there is a history in your team of avoiding giving feedback and side-stepping difficult conversations, leading to problems escalating and heated exchanges, try the following activity.

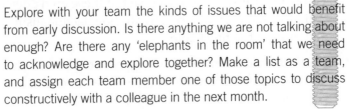

TEAM ACTIVITY
Tackle the tricky topics

Explore with your team the kinds of issues that would benefit from early discussion. Is there anything we are not talking about enough? Are there any 'elephants in the room' that we need to acknowledge and explore together? Make a list as a team, and assign each team member one of those topics to discuss constructively with a colleague in the next month.

2. Face-to-face is best

A face-to-face conversation is always the best approach for a difficult conversation. Emails are impersonal and open to misinterpretation. It is far too easy to fire off an email containing comments you would never say to the person's face. Sending an email also indicates to the recipient that you are fine with them emailing you back. The ensuing flurry of emails may not be the most effective way to progress the situation.

Even if there is a compelling reason to document everything in writing, you should still have the conversation in person first, then follow up with an email record of the content of the conversation so everyone is on the same page.

3. Be prepared

Before you meet for the important conversation, prepare. Decide on your objective—for example, is it to improve a relationship, resolve a problem or provoke learning?—and think about the best path to achieving it. Have all the relevant information available to you.

Consider carefully, before you meet with the employee, what the issue is, how it can be rectified and what the next step in the process is. Be as specific as you can and avoid generalities. It's a great idea to write a script for yourself beforehand, setting out the things you need to explore with the employee, the issue you want to address and the messages you need to deliver. Use specific examples of the problem at hand. Indicate that you want to resolve the issue, and invite the other person to explain their perspective. Think about what language you will use. For example, 'I want to talk with you about your interaction with customers' gives a very different impression to 'I need to talk to you about the way you intimidate customers into sales'. Always focus on the problem, not the person.

Consider in advance how the team member might respond to what you plan to say. If you anticipate that the person may become angry or upset, for example, have with you information about the employee counselling program. It is sometimes useful to have another person present for support or as a witness.

Before the meeting, practise saying aloud exactly what you want to say.

In the meeting, give the other person a real opportunity to explain their perspective. Really listen. Observe closely how they are communicating through their tone of voice and body language. Remember that they may feel defensive at first, so keep them talking with open-ended questions like, 'That's interesting. Why do you say that?' and 'What do you think needs to happen next?' Give them the opportunity to come up with ways to resolve the issue.

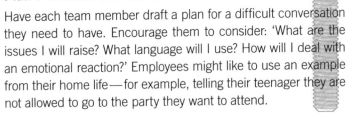

TEAM ACTIVITY
Plan a difficult conversation

Have each team member draft a plan for a difficult conversation they need to have. Encourage them to consider: 'What are the issues I will raise? What language will I use? How will I deal with an emotional reaction?' Employees might like to use an example from their home life—for example, telling their teenager they are not allowed to go to the party they want to attend.

4. Be fair and clear

It can be tempting to disguise the real reason you are meeting, to minimise the extent of the problem or understate the importance of the issue, to soften the blow. Don't! Avoiding the truth exacerbates the problem. We have seen too many performance reviews in which the supervisor intended to give a warning about a failure to improve, and the employee came out of the meeting feeling affirmed yet vaguely confused.

5. Be empathetic

Give some thought to the ideal time and location for the conversation, and give the employee sufficient notice of the subject of discussion. Some employees prefer to be able to leave work for the day immediately following a difficult conversation; others prefer to have the conversation at the start of the day so they can get it over with. Choose a neutral and private location to avoid interruption or observation by others.

Remember that the message you are conveying will be difficult for the employee to hear. No matter what words you use, what the other person actually takes away from the conversation will be influenced by their past experience, personality, culture, attitudes, fears, anxieties, assumptions and emotional intelligence. Choose your words carefully and be mindful of your tone, body language and other non-verbal communication. Focus on the employee's behaviour or actions, and avoid generalised or personal criticisms.

A conversation is a two-way process. Be aware of your own emotional reactions or 'triggers'. How are you going to manage your own emotions during the difficult conversation? Your aim should be to show detached concern during the meeting; if you start to feel overwhelmed, take a break.

6. Be prudent

However the conversation plays out, conclude by summarising what has been agreed or communicated, and what the next steps are.

Once the important conversation is over, document it. Record what was said and by whom, what the issues are and the agreed outcomes.

Following up the conversation in writing afterwards in a private file note or email to the person is a way of confirming your understanding of the discussion. It ensures there is no confusion or misunderstanding and confirms the mutual commitment you have made to taking future action. It also means you have a record of the conversation if the issues are not resolved.

TIP FOR MANAGERS
Keep good records

Get into the habit of documenting important conversations with a diary note or email (either to the other person or to yourself as a 'time-stamped' file note saved on your email system).

At the end of each week, reflect on those conversations and consider if any follow-up or further action is required.

TOOL #2
OFFER FACILITATED DISCUSSION, MEDIATION OR CONFLICT COACHING

Many of the dysfunctions that teams experience start out as a disagreement between two or more employees. The dysfunction itself can lead to conflict. Unless addressed early and carefully, conflict can spiral out of control and lead to factions, turf wars, inappropriate behaviour by individuals, loss of authority by the team's manager and other problems.

Three great tools to address conflict in the workplace are *facilitated discussion, mediation* and *conflict coaching.* A manager with good facilitation skills can run a facilitated discussion with some preparation. Mediation and conflict coaching are best delivered by a trained expert.

These interventions are practical, effective ways of de-escalating unhealthy conflict in the workplace. In the right circumstances, they are empowering and transformative. They assist employees to move forward with more positive working relationships, and lead to greater understanding and collaboration. They can also avoid the time, cost and disruption of more formal, legalistic processes.

What is a facilitated discussion?

A facilitated discussion is a voluntary, confidential discussion by the employees who are in conflict with each other, which is facilitated by their manager, another colleague or an external consultant.

A facilitated discussion is a flexible process. To assist with resolution, the facilitator can employ a range of methods and techniques, including a series of discussions over a period of time. The facilitator offers guidance and options to the participating employees on how they wish to resolve the conflict. In this advisory role, including actively guiding and prompting the employees to reach a solution, the facilitator usually remains impartial and doesn't take sides.

After the discussion, the facilitator may, when appropriate, share information about the conversations held and any agreement reached, with other relevant people at the workplace such as Human Resources. It is important that the parties in the facilitated discussion are aware of this in advance. An HR representative might also participate in some of the facilitated discussions, and guide or inform any ideas the parties have about a possible agreement.

In a facilitated discussion conducted by the manager, he or she can set objectives, test options and assist the employees with rules and guidance. The staff are exploring how to achieve the set objectives, rather than deciding what they want the objectives to be (unlike in mediation or coaching). Staff will be held to account for agreements they make in this process.

What is a mediation?

Like a facilitated discussion, a mediation is a voluntary, confidential discussion by employees who are in conflict with each other, although a mediation is a more formal process and is strictly confidential. A mediator will manage the discussion, giving each person in the mediation an opportunity to be heard and to hear what the other employee has to say. The mediation is future-focused, with employees themselves exploring how to work, communicate and behave together better. The mediator encourages—but does not force—the employees to reach agreement. The mediator can then help them to record the agreement, so they can refer to it later.

CHECKLIST
Key conditions for a successful mediation

☐ The mediator should be properly trained and experienced, and should be registered under the National Mediator Accreditation System.

☐ The mediator must be impartial.

☐ Confidentiality is key. What gets said in the mediation stays in the mediation.

☐ The parties (employees) must be open to considering the other person's point of view and to discussing ways forward.

Mediations and facilitated discussions:

- offer a circuit-breaker for conflict; they are an opportunity for employees to fix the situation before it gets any worse

- give employees time out of the workplace to 'clear the air' and express their perspectives in a safe space

- empower employees to be the drivers of the solution; employees themselves decide how they will resolve the conflict

- give employees the opportunity to determine an agreed framework for their ongoing working relationship

- demonstrate that the employer walks the talk on upholding its values such as safety and respect in the workplace

- are private

- can be quickly organised and completed.

Mediation or facilitated discussion will therefore be the right tool when the level of conflict is moderate, there are clearly identified issues that have tangible resolutions, and there is no significant disparity in the 'bargaining power' between the employees. It is important too that the employer is prepared to support the employees in abiding by the terms of any agreement they make, and to trust the mediator to run the process on a strictly confidential basis. Facilitated discussion and mediation work well only when the employees are capable of expressing themselves and representing their positions, they are open to the process and committed to trying to resolve the conflict, and they have some capacity to self-reflect and listen to the other's perspective.

TIP FOR MANAGERS
Stay in touch with consultants

If a colleague or external consultant is conducting the process, don't be afraid to talk with them about how it is going. They will know how much they can tell you about the *content* of what the employees are discussing, within the bounds of confidentiality. As the manager, you need to have confidence that the process is constructive and really helping the employees, and the team, get back on track.

What is conflict coaching?

Conflict coaching is a one-on-one process in which a trained conflict coach works with an employee to develop and enhance their competence and confidence to manage their interpersonal conflict, using a structured coaching model. Focused on the person's conflict management goals, conflict coaching is voluntary, confidential, pragmatic and user-friendly. It is possible for the conflict coach to work, separately and confidentially, with more than one employee involved in a workplace conflict.

Employees who participate in conflict coaching explore the triggers, impacts, assumptions and dynamics of the conflict from their perspective and the perspective of others in the conflict. The conflict coach helps the employee to a better understanding of their own situation, and explores what (if anything) they want to do to change their situation and how they feel they might do that. The employee thinks through their options, and the strategies and skills needed to manage and transform the conflict.

Underpinning conflict coaching is a belief that, with support and guidance from a coach, people are able to address their own problems. Conflict coaching is not therapy or counselling.

While it may not be suitable for conflict that has escalated to a point where relationships are irretrievably damaged (for example when there has been actual harm, threats or irretrievable loss of trust between the employees), conflict coaching can effectively address cases of entrenched conflict. As an alternative to a more formal process such as a misconduct investigation (Tool #4), conflict coaching can significantly minimise time, cost and damage to interpersonal relationships.

Conflict coaching can be the right tool in situations such as these:

- An employer would like to upskill an employee who has great potential but has also demonstrated deep-seated conflict behaviours.

- Two employees are in ongoing conflict with each other, and don't appear to be able to resolve the conflict themselves.

- Managers need assistance in preparing for a difficult conversation or managing a particularly challenging employee.

- Both parties to a facilitated discussion need help to increase their conflict management capability, self-awareness and goal-setting before they can effectively participate.

- Employees have participated in a formal misconduct investigation, and now need support to resolve the remaining conflict and explore how they will continue working together productively after the investigation.

TIP FOR MANAGERS
Stay present during the intervention

Remember that your leadership, oversight and guidance of employees must continue while the mediation, facilitated discussion and conflict coaching is being planned and delivered. You haven't contracted out of the day-to-day management of the team or the employees in conflict.

Chapter 15

THE FIX
ADDRESS UNCONSTRUCTIVE INDIVIDUAL BEHAVIOUR

IMPROVE BEHAVIOUR AND HOLD TEAM MEMBERS ACCOUNTABLE FOR THEIR CONDUCT.

If you have identified problematic individual behaviour and inappropriate conduct in your team, the Tools in this section are designed to help you address them and to improve accountability. They are about counselling and coaching the employee who is behaving badly, and investigating allegations of wrongdoing.

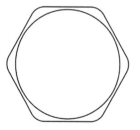 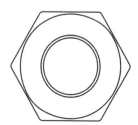

TOOL #3
COUNSEL THE BAD APPLE OR
UNPROFESSIONAL TEAM MEMBER

As discussed in chapter 3 on toxic personalities, Bad Apples have the capacity to damage team dynamics and undermine the manager's effectiveness and influence. Colleagues behaving unprofessionally (chapter 2) cause similar damage. To address this problematic behaviour, the manager—with the support of Human Resources, if needed—must personally inform the Bad Apple or unprofessional team member of the standard of conduct that applies to everyone in the team, what conduct they are engaging in that is breaching that standard, and what the Bad Apple must do to improve their conduct. The manager *must* then follow up and continue their supervision and counselling until the team member's conduct improves to a sufficient standard.

The manager's vigilant supervision of the Bad Apple's behaviour must continue until they improve. Remember, the manager is not expecting any more of the misbehaving employee than they expect from every employee! Being respectful and cooperative is the minimum standard that the whole team should meet. The Bad Apple is not being picked on or singled out—they are being called out, completely reasonably, on their bad behaviour.

If the Bad Apple does not improve their behaviour to a sufficient standard, they might need to be given a formal warning or face other disciplinary action. But let's start with informal counselling.

Step 1: Decide to give informal counselling

Managers, before you go in to address the bad behaviour, make sure you *know why* this conversation is important and what you need to achieve. Imagine the team without the unprofessional behaviour or the Bad Apple's negative influence: wouldn't that be a huge improvement for everyone?

Remind yourself at this stage that *it is your job* to maintain a reasonable standard of conduct and performance by the whole team. If you allow the Bad Apple or unprofessional team member to undermine the team's morale and functioning, the whole team will suffer. If you are nervous about insulting that person by counselling them, remember that the whole team is currently being offended and damaged, and they are (silently) looking to you to fix it. If you are nervous about creating risks for the organisation by having a difficult conversation with a volatile and malicious employee, remember the damage and risks that the Bad Apple is already causing: health and safety risks, productivity and culture risks, and possibly even legal and compliance risks.

If you are still loath to initiate the conversation, reflect on what may be holding you back. Do you fear conflict? Do you need more information? Do you need to practise the conversation with someone you trust, such as an HR manager, your own supervisor or a peer? Try taking the next step. Planning the conversation in detail will help you to consolidate your thoughts.

Step 2: Tell the Bad Apple or unprofessional team member what they must do to improve

As a manager, once you have decided to counsel an employee about their unconstructive conduct in the workplace, review the principles in Tool #1 for having an important conversation:

1. Be proactive.
2. Have the conversation face to face.
3. Be prepared.
4. Be honest and fair.

5. Be empathetic.

6. Be prudent.

As you plan for the conversation, remember that the Bad Apple may be driven by revenge, irrational dislike or genuine paranoid beliefs they may not be consciously anarchic. They are clearly feeling unmotivated and negative about work, as their default behaviour is overly critical, unhelpful and deliberately undermining. They may also be suffering from a personal crisis (see chapter 4), in which case you should still have the conversation but might consider seeking advice from HR first.

Once you have worked out what you need to say, consider having a practice conversation with a trusted peer or with HR before approaching the Bad Apple.

In the meeting, be open to what your team member may have to say. Do not assume that the employee will confess to, or apologise for, destructive behaviour. Be prepared for a strong reaction. The employee may:

- respond to you with anger, sarcasm, mockery, blame, denial or passive-aggressiveness
- sit there in stony silence, saying almost nothing
- use tears and pleading
- change the subject
- deflect the criticism back onto you or other members of the team
- pretend that everything is fine and there is no issue
- criticise you, management generally, or the organisation's current or past actions.

Even if the employee firmly disagrees that they have done anything inappropriate, your goal is to tell them what they must do or not do in future in order to meet your behavioural standards for the team. Be aware of your own emotional response, but stay focused.

TIP FOR MANAGERS
Be firm but fair in employee counselling

Although it may feel personal, there may be nothing you can do to change this person's perception of you. *Stay respectful, but remember that you are not there to be liked.* The important thing is to remain focused on the purpose of your discussion.

At the same time, *be yourself.* Sometimes managers think they need to act in an overly formal way. This can result in stiff, disengaged conversation and can hinder effective communication.

It may be that you find their bleak perspective understandable, if you are hearing about a dysfunctional workplace history stretching back to before your time, which you know has caused problems for the team. *Be empathetic and curious* about where they are coming from. Listen to what they have to say, but *be careful not to agree with their denial or defence* of their actions.

If the employee appears emotional or discloses personal issues during the meeting, *offer them access to the Employee Assistance Program* or other support.

Step 3: Follow up, follow up, follow up!

A Bad Apple or poorly behaving employee will not change their behaviour because of one conversation with you. In the first counselling meeting, make a time to meet again (say, in two weeks' time) to see how the employee is going.

You have determined some specific, identifiable things that the employee must do or not do, so keep an eye on the employee's conduct. If they breach your direction and behave badly again, you must address that breach *immediately.* The Bad Apple must understand that they can no longer behave in destructive, undermining ways — that there will be consequences for their actions, and that the first counselling session was not a one-off.

Step 4: Escalate to a formal disciplinary process if necessary

If the Bad Apple does not take advantage of the opportunity you have provided to address their behaviour, and they misbehave again, you should seek advice from Human Resources about escalating your approach. The organisation should have a code of conduct or disciplinary procedure that sets out the next steps.

Throughout this process, make sure that in your attempt to stay curious and empathetic, and to work constructively with the team member to improve their behaviour, you do not unwittingly take on their negativity. Dealing with difficult people can be draining and frustrating, so do look after yourself. Debrief with your supervisor, walk around the block, or do something that will enable you to regain a balanced perspective on the workplace (see chapter 23, on looking after yourself).

TIP FOR MANAGERS
Focus on the end game

Remember your goals!

- to hold the employee *accountable* for how they behave in the workplace

- to guide the employee to *change* their behaviour

- to affirm a *reasonable standard* of behaviour for the whole team

- to put the *organisation's values* into practice

- to demonstrate to the whole team your *integrity and fair approach*

- throughout the disciplinary process, follow the process to the letter (whatever it requires), keep records of what is happening, stay calm, and seek advice from HR or Legal if you start to struggle.

TOOL #4
GET THE ORGANISATION TO INVESTIGATE THE APPARENT MISCONDUCT AND DISCIPLINE THE WRONGDOER

A workplace investigation is a valuable Tool to have in your toolkit but one you may not often need to use. An investigation is usually undertaken only if the alleged behaviour, if proven, could breach the organisation's policies or code of conduct and the employer needs to consider taking disciplinary action for proven misconduct.

This could include, for example, bullying behaviour involving gossip (chapter 1), undermining others (chapter 3), breach of the organisation's conflict of interest policy (chapter 6), breach of the health and safety rules through overwork (chapter 12), or other wrongdoing outside the scope of this book. The organisation's policies might specify certain circumstances in which an investigation *must* be undertaken.

Sometimes other Tools have already been tried. The alleged wrongdoer may have already received informal counselling to encourage them to improve their conduct (Tool #3), conflict coaching or a mediation (Tool #2), training or team-building (tools #7 and #8). Despite these efforts, someone has made a complaint, or the employee has (again) acted in a way that may have breached the employer's policies and procedures.

An investigation of allegations of wrongdoing in the workplace is a process of inquiry and analysis that determines *findings of fact* about the allegations (what happened), and possibly also a finding of whether or not the employee has *breached the employer's policies and procedures* (whether what happened amounted to misconduct). The investigation should be conducted in a procedurally fair way, and the employer can rely on its findings to decide about taking disciplinary action or other appropriate remedies.

Commencing an investigation

If the circumstances are serious enough to warrant a formal misconduct investigation, it should be undertaken by an experienced investigator (either in-house or an external consultant).

Think through the following questions before you commence an investigation.

CHECKLIST
Key questions to consider before commencing an investigation

☐ Is an investigation necessary? Can you address the potential wrongdoing effectively using a quicker, less formal way, instead of commencing a formal misconduct investigation?

☐ What allegations should be investigated and what should not? (This determines the scope of the investigation.)

☐ Who is the best person to investigate? Do they have the impartiality, time, skill and capacity to run the investigation?

☐ What investigation process will be applied? How will the investigator ensure procedural fairness?

☐ Who will communicate with the parties and any witnesses? What information will employees be given during the course of the investigation?

☐ What information will the investigation report include? Who will it be provided to?

☐ If facts are proven, who will be responsible for making decisions about disciplinary action or other remedial steps that the employer should take?

☐ After the investigation, how will the outcome be communicated to the parties? What follow-up, counselling or other services will be offered to the employees? How will the organisation rebuild the damaged relationships between the employees and with the organisation?

Conducting an investigation in-house

Workplace investigations must be procedurally fair, planned, thorough and completed in a timely manner. If you wish to build your investigation skills, our comprehensive book *Workplace Investigations* (available through the Worklogic website) will guide you, as an in-house investigator, through the process.

To conduct a defensible investigation, the investigator must:

- know all the steps of an investigation and the investigation process. This includes how you will record information and what information you will provide to the parties during the process

- communicate these steps and the process to all the parties at the outset, as well as updating them during the investigation

- ensure that the parties' wellbeing is protected during the process, including access to a support person, and monitoring any health or capacity issues

- make sure that the allegations put to the respondent are clear and comprehensive so they can respond in detail to the complaint

- see the investigation through to a timely conclusion by avoiding unnecessary delay, while allowing for reasonable delays (such as for health reasons)

- consider all relevant evidence with impartiality, and give the parties the opportunity to respond to any key evidence or documents that arise during the investigation

- be able to support the findings you make from the evidence gathered and to apply the rules of evidence

- apply good judgement if a party attempts to block or corrupt the process—for example, by taking unapproved leave, refusing to answer questions or disputing the legitimacy of the investigation.

CHECKLIST
Procedural fairness 101

To be procedurally fair, an investigation requires at least the following:

☐ The respondent (the person responding to alleged misconduct) is provided with clear and specific allegations of fact, and the policy or procedure that they are accused of breaching.

☐ The respondent is given the opportunity to respond to those allegations and advised of the possible disciplinary outcomes that might follow if the allegations are proven.

☐ The investigator is impartial and unbiased. Also, they shouldn't have advised either of the parties before the investigation, or advised the manager of the team in which the wrongdoing allegedly happened.

☐ Confidentiality is maintained where possible.

☐ The investigation is conducted in a timely and thorough way.

☐ Participants are offered a support person.

☐ The investigation findings are made on the basis of the evidence collected.

☐ The respondent and the complainant both have the opportunity to consider and respond to evidence that contradicts their own.

Engaging an external investigator

Employers often decide to engage outside experts, who have the time, experience, skills and independence to conduct a defensible investigation. Professional investigators are used to the pressure and complexity of investigations, and have experience in determining procedural issues and challenges. If you decide to engage an external investigator, ensure they are properly experienced.

Many factors will influence your decision on whether an external investigator should be brought in. Here are the top three.

1. The seriousness of the allegations to be investigated

The more serious the allegations are, the more serious the consequences may be for the accused employee, if the allegations are proven. It's also likely that such allegations will be defended strongly, and for lawyers, unions and outside regulators (Fair Work Ombudsman, police, workplace health and safety regulators) to become involved. Litigation may follow, or charges against the organisation may be laid.

Because the investigation could potentially lead to disciplinary action, the requirements of natural justice and procedural fairness are critical. Any flaws in the investigation process could render any subsequent actions by the employer invalid.

Unless you are confident that the internal investigator will apply sufficient thoroughness, act in a timely and unbiased way, and provide procedural fairness to the parties, an external investigator is the safer option.

In addition, if the organisation is seeking legal advice about its liability, management of legal risk or defence of related proceedings, an investigation conducted *for the lawyer* (to inform the legal advice) can be covered by legal professional privilege. This means that the investigation, the evidence collected in it and the report of its findings could be protected from disclosure later in court.

2. Natural justice: the 'no bias' rule

Often, HR professionals and in-house risk, compliance and legal advisers have already dealt with the complaint and the people involved in the investigation. The person who would ordinarily investigate may therefore have a conflict of interest, or appear to the complainant or respondent to be biased. For example, the in-house lawyer may have advised one of the employees or their manager in the past about the situation, and appear to have taken sides.

3. The seniority of the complainant or respondent

If one of the parties is very senior, there may be a perception that the potential internal investigator does not have the requisite seniority or 'clout' to investigate the allegations, or feels uncomfortable given the obvious power imbalance (for example, a Human Resources business partner investigating the chief executive officer).

Once the investigation is complete

Formal investigations can themselves be stressful for employees. The goal of the investigation is not to 'heal' individuals or teams, but rather to determine and judge the facts. Once the complaint has been investigated, what should employers do to help the team to repair itself? How can the employer help employees to rebuild relationships and get back to work?

The *individual interventions* that are most successful in improving workplace culture focus on the parties' emotions. They include facilitated discussion and mediation (Tool #2) to encourage parties to come to a mutual understanding of their colleagues' feelings; offering counselling; and disciplinary action to indicate a strong commitment to ethical conduct in the workplace. After an investigation, *team interventions* should focus on collaboration and a reduction in alienation of particular individuals, including through:

- training about bullying, conflict management and being an active bystander

- using employee feedback mechanisms to help identify problem areas

- team-building activities (Tool #7) to build a sense of openness, trust and accountability

- training managers to intervene, to handle workplace disputes confidently and to set a model example for fellow colleagues (Tool #11).

Chapter 16

THE FIX
DEVELOP THE TEAM'S CHARACTER AND CONNECTIONS

DEVELOP ETHICAL CHARACTER AND A SENSE OF COMMUNITY.

The Tools in this section are designed to build the team members' skills in self-reflection, mindfulness, autonomy and ability to relate to one another. It includes practical ways to think about strategic recruitment and run team-building activities.

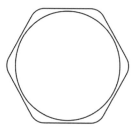
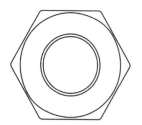

TOOL #5
NEXT HIRE

Sometimes the mix of people in the team is just not quite right; the balance is off. Either there is a very strong influence that is pulling the team in a direction it doesn't want to go, or there is something missing, in skills, demographics, roles or ways of operating.

We all know what a significant difference one new person can make to a team's culture and operating style. When an opportunity arises to *recruit or transfer* someone new into the team, take advantage of it. Use the process for selecting the new hire strategically to nudge the team to be more functional. Yes, it's only one person in a team of many, and one person can't singlehandedly correct a dysfunctional dynamic, but they can make a noticeable difference.

If the team is skewed in its values...

You might have one strong personality in the team who is corrupting the team's dynamic—such as a Bad Apple (chapter 3) or a racist (chapter 7)—and no one strong enough to offer an alternative for how the team engages with each other and approaches the work.

Placing a strong emphasis on values is a good strategy for *all* recruitment, not only when you want to influence the team dynamic. Values-based recruitment has gained traction in recent years, along with recognition that values are the 'glue' that holds teams together, particularly in tough times and in times of change.

First, make sure you have a sound understanding of the values you want to encourage in the team, and the types of behaviours you hope the successful candidate will exhibit, which underpin your recruitment framework. Then make sure these are reflected in job advertisements, job descriptions, shortlisting criteria and methods, interview questioning, and interview assessment and scoring.

TIP FOR MANAGERS
Craft good interview questions

Here are some interview questions you might ask to focus on values and assess culture fit:

- What sort of team culture do you work best in?

- How would you describe the values of our organisation, based on what you've seen? What is it about these values that appeals to you?

- Tell me about a time when you worked with a company where you felt your values weren't a strong fit with that company's values. Why was it a bad fit, and what did you do about it?

- Do you have any advice for one of your past bosses?

You might ask these interview questions in order to assess the candidate's strengths as a team player:

- How have you had to adapt your style to work with different types of teams?

- You are part of a project team with an upcoming deadline, but the team has been unable to agree on the strategy or project plan to meet the deadline. How might you move things along?

- In the next five minutes, teach me something I'm not likely to know already.

If the team is skewed in its role preferences...

The team might need someone who prefers to play a particular role, in order to function at its best. For example, it may have plenty of visionaries and creatives, but no one who is interested in operationalising ideas, keeping projects on track or bringing projects to completion. An imbalance in the employees' preferences for the role they play within the team can be a contributing factor to Complete Chaos (chapter 11) or overwork (chapter 12).

Considering each team member's role preferences, and any gaps that exist in the team as a whole, can help you identify what 'role' strengths, as well as technical skills and functional abilities, you should look for in the next person you hire or bring into the team.

TEAM ACTIVITY
Identify preferred team roles

If you suspect there's something about the team makeup that is leading to missed deadlines, projects stalling, stale ideas or uncoordinated effort, consider applying Dr Meredith Belbin's Team Roles theory. In the exercise Belbin for Teams®, each team member completes a short questionnaire that indicates their role preferences. The nine Belbin Team Roles are clusters of behaviour that are displayed in the workplace: Resource Investigator, Teamworker, Coordinator, Plant, Monitor/Evaluator, Specialist, Shaper, Implementer and Completer/Finisher. You can then look at the Team Roles across the group, work out what is missing, and learn more about how you operate as individuals and as a group.

A similar system of organisational development is Team Management Systems (TMS), developed by Australian scientists Charles Margerison and Dick McCann.

If the team is skewed in its demographics ...

Yes, we're talking about diversity and inclusion (chapter 7). The good news is that many organisations are taking a much more creative and strategic approach to ensure they attract a diverse range of candidates. For example, they are taking a different approach to advertising. Think outside the box and advertise roles outside traditional media outlets. Innovative recruitment videos on YouTube featuring a diverse group of staff have been known to go viral. Or you can seek out recruitment schemes run by community groups, not-for-profit organisations and universities, which encourage the employment of people from traditionally underemployed groups and give you access to a more diverse group of candidates.

Ensure unconscious bias isn't creeping into your recruitment decisions. As discussed in chapter 7, unconscious bias is a real danger to merit-based and fair decision making in recruitment. Things you can do to counter it include:

- training in unconscious bias for managers and hiring decision makers
- de-identifying candidates' personal details from applications in the first round of recruitment, so their name, gender, age and cultural background are not taken into consideration (even unconsciously) in the shortlisting process
- online testing of unconscious bias—for example, the free tests on Harvard University's Project Implicit website.

TIP FOR MANAGERS
Be thorough in assessing candidates

Shadowing

Some prospective employers invite the shortlisted candidates to 'shadow' a member of the team for an afternoon, attending an event or meeting, then seek feedback from the team member or even an outside stakeholder on that individual's skills and traits.

Referees

When speaking with referees, go beyond functional and skills-based questions. Explore how the candidate acts under pressure, so you can get a sense of their ability to manage emotion and stress triggers. You may be able to pinpoint behaviours that wouldn't be helpful for team dynamics—blaming, anger or manipulative behaviour. You may get a sense of their level of emotional maturity by exploring how well they respond to receiving guidance and feedback.

Skills and personality testing

Including a psychometric test for candidates to undertake at some stage in your recruitment process can provide insightful data. Before using psychometric testing, know what you are testing for, such as resilience, collegiality, values, or perhaps the candidate's preferred role in the team (using a tool such as Belbin, discussed above). Choose a test that fits your particular needs.

Welcome the new recruit and set them up for success

If you hired the new recruit partly because of their values or the way you expect they will interact with the team, don't be afraid to tell them this. A person's strength of character, sound values or preference for being a Monitor/Evaluator or Implementer, for example, are all great benefits that they bring to the team, as are their experience and expertise in the relevant subject matter, their ability to speak different languages or their knowledge of logistics.

Of course, you won't have chosen the person 'only because' their ethnic, cultural or religious background or gender helped redress an imbalance in diversity. No one likes to feel they were hired because of their personal characteristics rather than their abilities, so it is not appropriate to highlight this.

Once the new employee has been hired, induction should be a time for discussing, exploring and confirming in a meaningful way the organisation's values, and the emphasis your team puts on cooperation, respect and accountability. Members of the team can be invited to participate in the induction process through an informal social gathering, such as a morning tea, and a one-on-one meeting with a colleague to talk through the new employee's role and how they like to work.

TEAM ACTIVITY
Connect with the new starter

Once the new starter has joined, consider having a conversation about the strengths of the team in the next team meeting. What do the team members enjoy about the team dynamic? What do we do really well? What strengths can we build on? In the past year, when did the team members feel proud? When have we felt most connected with one another? What has been fun? How do we celebrate success? What do we want to do more of?

Talking about the way you work together will help the new employee to understand and engage with the team. It will also remind the team, in a future-focused and constructive way, what is working.

TOOL #6
DEVELOP SELF-REFLECTION IN THE WHOLE TEAM

When we are called in to help fix a team that has been shattered for years, the most common thing we hear from employees is, 'That's just the way it is around here'. At the heart of that comment is a very depressing assumption: 'I can't do anything about the awful way we are working together.' Perhaps the employee knows what might shift the dial, but they don't have the energy to try. Perhaps they think they lack the necessary influence to achieve it. Perhaps they have tried in the past and met with resistance.

A key ingredient to changing a poor team dynamic for the better is *the right outlook* of the majority of the team. This requires the team members to build their abilities to *observe* what is going on in the team, *self-reflect and imagine* a better way of working together; to *be mindful* by being present and undistracted for yourself and others; and to *feel a sense of autonomy*, believing you can do something to influence the situation for the better.

Observe, self-reflect, imagine

Self-reflection is not easy. People are inherently unable to be objective about themselves and their own contribution to dysfunctional situations. There are various ways you can help them to do this.

One approach is to ask one employee (who is able to be brave and honest while respectful) to *observe a team meeting*. At the end of the meeting, ask them to share with everyone their observations about how the team interacted. For example: Who used most of the airtime? Did anyone fail to contribute at all? Was every person present engaged and listening? What was the feel of the room (tense, open, encouraging…)? What can we learn from this exercise? How might we do things differently next time?

Another approach is to bring in a team of *actor/facilitators*, who use role plays and improvisation to model positive and negative teamwork scenarios. Seeing others act out scenarios in an engaging, entertaining and non-confrontational manner, then participating in a facilitated discussion about what we've learned about ourselves and how our team operates, can be very effective.

Then there's Mooski, a delightful team experience we created. Built on the latest research from organisational psychologists and business schools into resilience, motivation, innovation and workplace culture, Mooski is a smartphone-enabled team-building program. Over three weeks, colleagues get to know one another better, and reflect as individuals on their work relationships, values and strengths.

Mindfulness

Mindfulness as a concept has been around for thousands of years. In recent times, employers have recognised the relevance and importance of mindfulness to the workplace and to worker wellbeing.

This might be partly due to the rise of new technology, which should enhance the interface between our personal and business lives and give us more flexibility and control, but can instead lead to an expectation that staff will be available 24/7. With email and social media accessible all the time and wherever we are, it can be very difficult to find the head space to stop and really think.

Mindfulness means focusing your awareness on the present moment, while calmly acknowledging and accepting your own feelings and sense of being physically present. Being mindful lets you move beyond your immediate emotional reactions to be much more effective. You can be aware of what you're sensing and feeling at every moment, without interpretation or judgement.

Practising mindfulness in your everyday interactions will increase your sense of calm and your appreciation of the things that matter. It will let you approach the work with openness and self-awareness. Being mindful and present for your colleagues will help stimulate real conversations and enrich your work relationships. To do this, you need to see clearly and calmly, and not be blinded by emotion or petty concerns from the past.

To encourage your team to take a mindful approach at work, you could:

- offer a lunchtime training session on the practice of mindfulness and the benefits it can offer

- start a meeting with one minute of deep breathing in silence

- ask questions in the team meeting that encourage mindful reflection, such as 'What did people notice about how we worked together this week?' or 'Are people feeling connected with their work at the moment?'

- explore the possibility of running a yoga class before work, either with an instructor (if your workplace has the budget) or using a recorded session

- organise an exercise aimed at being present for one another, such as going for a walk.

TIP FOR MANAGERS
Be open to mindfulness

Not everyone is open to concepts such as mindfulness. Some people find it confronting to talk about feelings or personal experience. Some members of your team might feel embarrassed, or might not want to let themselves be vulnerable in front of one another. They might try to dismiss the concepts as 'new age' or religious.

There are indirect and gentle ways to introduce the concept of mindfulness, such as going for a walk together and deep breathing as part of a wellbeing program the organisation is offering.

Autonomy

All of us want to have control of our own lives and, to the extent that it is possible, choose what we do and how we do it. Of course, when you work for someone else, this isn't always possible. In some roles, employees must follow a set process rigorously and comply with strict requirements. For example, factory workers often do repeated set tasks in strict order and electricians have stringent compliance requirements. In some fields, such as manufacturing, finance and health sectors, there are strict regulations to ensure that risks are controlled. Operating within the parameters of the law or regulations is an important part of working in those settings.

Although we usually don't have much control over the work we do, we can always choose the way we approach the tasks and the attitude we bring to work. A person's mindset makes a significant difference to how they experience each day, and how they react to each event.

For example, say a colleague whom you don't really like sends an abrupt email one Monday morning. You immediately think, 'What a loser! Doesn't she realise how rude and petty she sounds all the time?' If someone you like and respect sent that same abrupt email, you might think, 'Wow, that issue must really matter. Perhaps she is getting pressure from the top on that project. I wonder what I can do to help.'

TEAM ACTIVITY
Create ideal attributes

Sit down as a team and brainstorm a list of the attributes of the ideal team member—the type of person you all want to work with. For example, it might include: helpful, knowledgeable, available to help, positive. Put all those attributes on a poster in the team's workspace. Each week, choose one of those attributes to focus on. All the team members can 'try on' that attribute for the week. You might like to discuss what you noticed about your team members' actions that embodied that characteristic.

Everyone suffers at times in their career, when things going on around them feel depressing, inefficient or unfair, and this is particularly true for members of a broken or toxic team. We all face shocks, boredom, conflicts and fears. The question is, who do you choose to be in the difficult moments? Where do you choose to direct your efforts? What sort of co-worker do you choose to be for your team each day? Authentic, supportive and creative? Perhaps brave, listening and reflective? Energetic and purposeful?

Invite your team to choose their attitude. We're not suggesting that the hurtful things that happen around you don't matter. We're suggesting you reframe the experience as a challenge to meet, rather than a reason to give up.

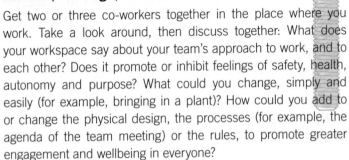

TEAM ACTIVITY
Refresh, redesign, renovate!

Get two or three co-workers together in the place where you work. Take a look around, then discuss together: What does your workspace say about your team's approach to work, and to each other? Does it promote or inhibit feelings of safety, health, autonomy and purpose? What could you change, simply and easily (for example, bringing in a plant)? How could you add to or change the physical design, the processes (for example, the agenda of the team meeting) or the rules, to promote greater engagement and wellbeing in everyone?

Now you have some ideas, what could you do to implement them? If you need approval to make a certain change, how can you seek it?

A final note for the sceptics. If you're thinking that these quiet, thoughtful, self-reflective moments are a waste of time for you or your team, consider the brain science. Studies have shown that mindfulness and meditation can increase subjective wellbeing and reduce emotional reactivity. Employees who feel a sense of autonomy have higher job satisfaction (+10 per cent), perform better (+5 per cent), and are more innovative (+8 per cent). A positive mindset also has clear positive consequences for employees' goal achievement.

TOOL #7
BUILD THE TEAM'S CONNECTIONS

Often, when teams have been through the ringer of conflict, trauma, toxic behaviour and unethical practice, they don't even feel like a team. They feel like a bunch of individuals who are each trying to complete their assigned tasks, in the same physical space, with the least amount of interaction. All they are likely to share is a certain level of defensiveness and bitterness, and perhaps time spent on job-hunting websites!

Even damaged teams can benefit from investing some time together, to get to know each other as individuals, to build connections and to share ideas. When the employer invites a team to do an activity together, that is not about being productive (making widgets, selling products, treating patients...), but is about building the team, it sends a good message. It says to the team: *we value you, and your experience of this workplace matters.*

TIP FOR MANAGERS
Repair the team before building the team

A team-building exercise is not the same as a *team repair* exercise. Offering a team-building activity to a team that is grieving from a recent traumatic event, in a very high state of conflict, or experiencing high levels of toxic behaviour, is *not* an appropriate first step. It would appear that you are trying to paper over the real problem. Teams with skeletons in the closet, high conflict or Bad Apples risk having the same destructive behaviours and dynamics emerge unpleasantly in the middle of the exercise.

A recent traumatic event or high state of conflict should be addressed directly first—through mediation, facilitated discussion

(continued)

TIP FOR MANAGERS
Repair the team before building the team (*cont'd*)
or conflict coaching (Tool #2), counselling or discipline of a wrongdoer (Tool #3), and/or supporting the team through personal crises (Tool #13) *before* team-building is offered.

Short team-building exercises can be carried out in or near the workplace, or in an informal setting away from work. Involving a bigger time commitment, offsite activities give team members more time to get to know one another and tend to be more memorable.

Some require a budget. If you have zero budget for this sort of activity, explore the outside interests and skills of the team members. Could you learn a new skill from a colleague? Visit someone's farm? Undertake a project for a charity for which a team member volunteers? Be creative about what you can do for free.

The content of the team-building activity you choose will depend on the 'building' you think the team needs. Do the team members need to *get to know each other better*? Do they need to try *new ways of approaching challenges*? Perhaps they just need some *time to relax*, 'play' and have a laugh together.

In our experience, it's constructive to engage all employees at the outset and draw out their creative ideas about what the team-building program might entail. Rather than asking in a team meeting—when certain people often dominate the airtime—consider emailing the team a short online survey or put a suggestion box in the break room. Give them a number of options for different activities, then ask them to select their top three and also to propose a fourth (something new that is not on the list). Try to avoid traditional competitive sports, as this can greatly enliven some people and alienate others! Golf, rock climbing and obstacle courses will exclude older workers,

workers with different abilities or those who are afraid of heights! The last thing you want is to send a message that some members of the team don't belong.

Based on the employees' votes, leaders choose the team-building activity that will be offered (perhaps two or three different activities across a large group of people).

TIP FOR MANAGERS
Select groups strategically

When designing team-building exercises to take place out of the office, if you are dividing the team into smaller groups, selection is key! Remember that you want your employees to build relationships with people they haven't yet got to know at work.

Getting to know you

Activities that give employees an opportunity to get to know one another better (including their talents and skills) are particularly helpful where team members have been thrown together, as in a restructure or a merger between companies or teams, or when a long-absent employee returns. These activities are non-competitive fun and engage the team in a pastime they might not have tried before.

The types of activity that will resonate with your team will depend on its culture and composition. You might consider a barista course, a cooking course, a guided walk around street art of the city or a public gallery, an art workshop, 'barefoot bowls' at your local bowling club, helping out on a farm, serving breakfast at a homeless shelter, a walk around a local park or a trivia afternoon.

If the activity is conducted offsite, do a risk assessment in advance to protect occupational health and safety.

New approaches

The aim of these creative, problem-solving exercises, which have been around for a long while, is to build connections between team members where they wouldn't otherwise exist. They can include a competitive element, be organised at very low cost and have an immediate impact, as we see in the following case study.

CASE STUDY
CREATIVE CAKE CUTTING

At the Germaine Design Agency, Mandy is a quiet, diligent employee with a young family. She is a strong performer, but keeps to herself and isn't really well known by her workmates, partly because she works hard throughout the day and leaves at 3 pm. At a workplace retreat, the staff are broken into teams and asked to solve a series of brainteasers, including, 'What is the maximum number of slices of cake you can cut if you have a round cake and can only make four straight cuts?'

Several of the teams propose that if you cut a cake the traditional way, with all four cuts through the centre and crossing in the middle, you get eight slices.

One team says that if you cut the cake in a checkerboard pattern, cutting it into thirds one way then in thirds the opposite way, you can get nine slices.

Mandy works out that if you cut the cake in two, arrange the pieces alongside each other, cut the cake again, arrange the four pieces alongside each other again and so on, the maximum number of slices you can create is sixteen. There are lots of laughs, with some participants start joking about breaking the rules of the challenge and eating their cake. Mandy's team wins the challenge and her workmates look at Mandy in a new light.

> A few weeks later when looking for 'fresh eyes' to brainstorm a solution to a tricky customer request, a manager remembers Mandy's creative approach to the cake-cutting challenge, and asks for her input on the project.

This kind of exercise can be done in a short time either at work or as part of a longer work retreat or planning day. It is aimed at exploring team dynamics, putting people in roles they don't usually fill, working with different people across the team.

One way to get short team-building exercises really working is to give your team a mission! As Daniel Pink explains in his book *Drive* (2011), nothing bonds a team like a shared mission (whether you are competing with other teams or simply against the clock). If you put some care into choosing teams that include people who don't normally work together, and ensure you split up any 'factions' or close friends within the team, a mission will let the employees try on different roles and see each other in a new light.

Here are some 'mission'-type team-building activities:

- **A paper plane competition**. Whose plane can fly the greatest distance? The highest? Whose has the most creative design?

- **Marshmallow challenge**. Who can build the tallest tower given 20 strands of uncooked spaghetti, a metre of masking tape, a metre of string and one marshmallow? The team has 20 minutes to build the tallest freestanding structure they can and the marshmallow must rest unassisted on top of the structure for at least 30 seconds (see the TED talk by Tom Wujec).

- **Auteur experiment**. Give teams two hours to plan, film and edit a short film about your organisation in a particular style (such as a comedy, children's, sci-fi or cooking show).

- **Design challenge**. Ask your teams to design a coat of arms or logo for the department.

- **Scavenger hunt**. Organise your employees into small teams for a photographic scavenger hunt in the streets around the office. Award a prize to the first team that comes back with photos of:

  » a member of your team with a busker, outside a sushi shop and up a tree

  » a team member standing next to an iconic statue, in the same pose as the subject

  » the whole team sitting on a particular tram, bus or train (such as the 333 to Kings Cross)

  » a particular book in the library

  » the whole team eating a pie

  » the whole team with a uniformed police officer.

  Photographic scavenger hunts are a great thing to use when you have teams in different locations, as they can be completed on smartphones simultaneously in locations anywhere around the world. Teams have until a particular time of day to upload or share photographs (or video) with the person judging the competition.

After the team-building exercise, reflect together on what the team enjoyed. Formal identification of 'what we learned about each other's strengths and working styles' can be a bit laboured, but some light-hearted discussion about the most enjoyable parts of the day, what surprised you about the team's approaches to the challenges, and whether there's anything we'd like to do differently as a team in future, can be beneficial.

Chapter 17
THE FIX
ALIGN WITH VALUES

DEVELOP A TEAM IN WHICH EVERYONE IS JUDGED ON MERIT AND LIVES THE ORGANISATION'S VALUES.

If your goal is to develop a diverse team that lives and breathes the organisation's values, then apply the Tools in this section. They include ideas for bringing the values to life, and some practical steps you can take to encourage diversity and inclusion in your workplace, if this is part of your organisation's values. You can also develop the team's openness to feedback and self-improvement.

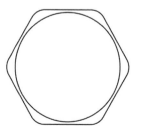
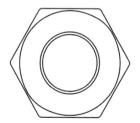

Chapter 17

THE FIX
ALIGN WITH VALUES

DEVELOP A TEAM IN WHICH EVERYONE
IS JUDGED ON MERIT AND LIVES THE
ORGANISATION'S VALUES.

TOOL #8
DIVERSITY AND INCLUSION INITIATIVES

The business case for a diverse and inclusive workplace is clear. Diversity (a mix of demographics in the team's makeup) and inclusion (everyone being able and welcome to contribute) can generate innovation through the exchange of varied ideas. Employees will be more engaged if they feel valued, no matter what their cultural, ethnic or religious background. Productivity increases. Employees, as well as products, services and advertising, are more likely to be representative of (and appeal to) customers. Colleagues are more likely to treat one another with respect. The Inclusion@Work survey in 2017 found that, in Australia, employees who work in an inclusive team are 19 times more likely to be 'very satisfied' with their job.

The diversity of the leaders of organisations is important too. Recent research reported in the *Harvard Business Review* found that organisations that have leaders who have both inherent diversity (traits the person was born with) and acquired diversity (diversity of experience) were more innovative and performed better than those organisations that didn't. Those companies were 45 per cent more likely to report that their market share had grown over the previous year, and 70 per cent more likely to report that they had captured a new market. Here are five steps to consider.

1. The minimum standard: Combat unreasonable discrimination, give reasonable consideration to flexible working arrangements, and make reasonable adjustments

If you have identified that the team needs some work on the diversity and inclusion front, start by *immediately* addressing any overt racism, homophobia, sexism and other prejudice.

Such conduct is unlawful, and the organisation (as well as the managers and colleagues) have a legal obligation to address this unsafe, unethical and damaging situation in the workplace. See Tool #3, 'Counsel the Bad Apple or unprofessional team member' and Tool #4, 'Get the organisation to investigate the apparent misconduct, and discipline the harasser'.

Employers are legally responsible for preventing and stopping unreasonable discrimination, which occurs when someone is not employed at all, or is denied an opportunity or advancement, or otherwise treated unfavourably, on grounds that are irrelevant to their ability to do the job. Research to understand which groups have most typically been disadvantaged resulted in the list of 'protected attributes' that are now protected in equal opportunity and anti-discrimination laws.

Under current legislation, organisations and managers are required to give reasonable consideration to requests from staff for flexible working arrangements, where an employee requests such an arrangement to accommodate their carer responsibilities. If a request is made, it is valuable for the whole team to engage in a discussion about how the work can be done (within the bounds of confidentiality). It may be as simple as checking the proposed time of a meeting with all participants before it is booked. Discussions like this also foster a culture in which all team members are supported to work flexibly as the need arises.

Employers must also make reasonable adjustments to the workplace so that people with special needs or different abilities can participate fully. For example, this could include the ergonomics of the workstation, the use of technology or changes to the layout of the meeting room.

2. Reflect on the whole organisation: Where are you at?

In forward-thinking contemporary workplaces, rather than just meeting minimum standards of avoiding discrimination, a more positive approach is taken. Whereas *anti-discrimination* focuses on not unfairly disadvantaging staff and job applicants, *diversity and inclusion* have the positive aspiration of creating a workplace culture, teams and individuals with a wide range of beliefs, styles, backgrounds and experiences. In such workplaces, everyone is encouraged, valued and respected for who they are (rather than simply being 'tolerated').

Many factors influence the organisation's embrace (or not) of diversity and inclusion in its strategy and operations, such as the organisation's size, leaders' priorities, values, industry, Human Resources capacity, geographic locale and purpose, as well as overall workplace culture. Each of these factors influences the real support, visibility and viability of such initiatives.

3. Check your systems and processes

You don't need to be a diversity expert to conduct an audit of the processes and procedures that affect the team. Cast a critical eye and review them for potential discriminatory impact, direct and indirect.

- Are the criteria that are (informally) embedded in your processes skewed to favour certain groups in ways that are unrelated to job performance? An example might be assessing team members' commitment by whether they show up at the pub for Friday night drinks. Such an approach would unfairly affect how you view staff with parental or carer responsibilities, for a start.

- Do your policies make clear statements of values and support of diversity and inclusion initiatives, such as flexible work and multi-faith end-of-year celebrations?

- Do you always ask the same team members for their opinion? Why not throw some different voices into the mix?

- Where do you advertise for jobs in your team? Who is applying for the jobs you advertise? If you are getting no applicants from certain ethnic groups, or getting applications only from young people, ask yourself why. Is there something about the job design, the recruitment process or the culture of the team that is encouraging or discouraging certain groups of people?

- What visual images are chosen to represent your company, its staff and its customers? Do those images demonstrate any favouritism towards certain types of individual? For example, if the advertisements for your company's products all show blond Caucasian families (mum, dad and two kids), who might you be discouraging?

4. Check yourself: making fair and transparent decisions

Assumptions about another person, based on observable personal characteristics that are unrelated to their merit, have the potential to be very damaging.

CASE STUDY
SALESPERSON SLIP-UP

Amelia has purchased a new car, and attends an appointment at the dealership with a salesperson who is going to run her through the car's features when she collects it. Arriving at the dealership, Amelia is greeted by Lorena, who leads her through the showroom. Amelia is about to thank Lorena for showing her to the vehicle, when she realises that it is Lorena who will be demonstrating the features of the new car to her. Somehow, Amelia had just assumed that the salesperson would be male.

Lorena is a great guide, explaining the car's key features in a clear and user-friendly way. She answers all Amelia's questions. At that moment, Amelia feels silly, but luckily her assumption did not affect her decision making or the way she spoke to Lorena. Things might have been different had Amelia been the hiring manager for the dealership, and Lorena a potential applicant for the position.

If you are a manager, you will have significant influence over decisions that advantage some people over others. It's important to be aware of key work processes where this occurs. They include recruitment; access to training, coaching and further education; career opportunities, including promotions and special projects; salary setting, bonuses, pay increases and others rewards and recognition; access to overtime or preferred work patterns or shifts; and selection for redundancy or contract renewal. To test yourself for unconscious bias (described in chapters 7 and 16), ask yourself:

- Are a variety of people involved in decision making, or do you surround yourself with people with similar views to your own?

- Are you truly being independent about how you best utilise and reward all the talents, skills and experiences of your colleagues? Is it possible that your criteria are inadvertently skewed?

- If you are a manager or decision maker, get the data and check the statistics. What are the demographics of the people you have been employing and promoting? Who is progressing on your watch? If your decisions always lead to people from the same group being successful, it is more likely that there is something amiss with your decision making than that a whole 'other' population lacks merit. For example, when was the last time you promoted someone who was on maternity leave, who worked part-time or who was over 55 years old? Also look at employees' starting salaries, pay increments, progression speed, training spend, overtime and access to development opportunities such as managing a project.

- Consider applying an online tool to check your own implicit biases, such as Harvard University's Implicit Association Test on the Project Implicit website. As part of a professional development program, you could invite your whole team to complete the test, and discuss together what you learned about yourselves.

If you make decisions about conferring benefits on individuals, such as recruitment or promotion, try masking the demographic details of the applicants so decision makers are comparing anonymised applicants only on their genuine merits. Studies have shown that identical résumés with different names (such as Peter Jamison vs Farouk Kamal) are routinely treated differently, and the applicant with a Caucasian name is more likely to be successful.

TIP FOR MANAGERS
Balance transparency and confidentiality

When you make a decision that confers advantage or disadvantage, document your criteria and your reasoning, and consider sharing these with your team (if you can do this without betraying confidentiality). Transparency minimises misunderstandings about motives, criteria and standards. It also provides an opportunity for coaching team members on how they can position themselves for a better outcome next time.

5. Increase inclusion in your team

Building a culture of diversity and inclusion is the responsibility of the whole team. Here are eight ways to make your team (and you) more inclusive:

- *Be curious!* Our natural inclination is to hang out with those who are like us, and who reinforce our established thoughts and opinions. Take the trouble to encourage your team to be more curious about others' views and values.

- In meetings, go around the table and give everyone the opportunity to contribute. Be aware of *sharing voice time*. In some cultures, subordinates speak only if a more senior person asks them a direct question, or there is a silence after one person finishes speaking. Make sure each member of your team has respectful insight around this.

- Encourage team members to *seek ideas and opinions* from many people (or different people) in the team when collaborating and consulting on a project.

- Are team members (and you) *flexible and supportive about how, when and where the work gets done?* Measure outcomes, not hours spent 'at the desk'.

- When speaking, do your team members (and you) put the *person first*, and not the differentiating feature (so, for example, 'a person with a disability' not 'a disabled person')?

- Encourage everyone at work to use *language that is respectful, accurate and relevant to everyone.* Some language can marginalise certain groups and treat them with contempt. People who think their colleague 'just can't take a joke' usually belong to those groups about which jokes are rarely made.

- Make sure you hold *inclusive social functions*. It's not hard to include dishes that are halal, kosher or vegetarian. When planning work events and social get-togethers, include employees from a variety of different cultural and religious backgrounds to benefit from their experiences and knowledge.

- Help team members to reflect on who they socialise with, inside and outside of work, so they are inclusive in social activities, and no one feels excluded or marginalised.

TOOL #9
MAKE SURE THE ORGANISATION'S VALUES AND BEHAVIOURAL EXPECTATIONS ARE KNOWN, CLEAR, UNDERSTOOD AND REAL

At the heart of *nearly all the team dysfunctions* outlined in this book is a failure of values. For example, unhealthy competition (chapter 10) privileges profit over the wellbeing of staff. Weak managers (chapter 9) lack integrity when they fail to hold the team accountable for their performance and conduct. Nepotism (chapter 6) damages the fairness of decision making, and toxic personalities (chapter 3) are fundamentally unkind and dishonest. We could go on …!

One of the core foundations of rebuilding and reinforcing the values of the team is the existence of a values-based culture of the whole organisation. The organisation's values should be a blueprint for employee behaviour, and a guide for making strategic and operational decisions, and should set the company apart from its competitors. They describe the core ethics or principles the company will abide by, no matter what.

In practice, company values are particularly useful when deciding between two or more strategic or operational options—decisions as common as choosing between potential contractors in a procurement process, deciding on the branding of a product or recruiting a new employee. Stated values are also helpful when the issue being decided is in the 'grey' area of ethics, and there's no clear right or wrong answer.

Strong, clearly articulated values inspire our best efforts and also constrain the actions of the organisation and its people. Your organisational values also underpin your organisation's code of conduct and policies, which clearly define acceptable behaviour at your organisation, and are key tools for managing inappropriate behaviour and misconduct.

Organisational values must make an honest statement of what the company believes in. If employees see a disconnect between what the organisation says are its values and what happens in reality, cynicism will result. Similarly, values that do not resonate with staff or reflect your company's culture and aspirations can actually demotivate employees, alienate customers, and undermine the credibility of leaders and managers.

Anyone in the organisation can initiate a focus on organisational values, although authorising and resourcing a values project will be the responsibility of managers and leaders.

Why define organisational values?

Table 17.1 outlines the benefits of discussing and confirming our organisational values.

Table 17.1: the benefits of discussing and confirming values

Discussing and confirming our values helps us to:	We therefore gain:
Create better understanding of the vision we're working towards	Clarity
Help people to work better together	Cooperation
Create the 'glue' that binds the team together	Coherence
Focus our attention on the right issues	Focus
Create greater value for all the stakeholders	Outcomes
Have a reference point when making decisions in the 'grey areas'	Guidance

If your organisation developed its values 10 years ago—as a clue, the old favourites tend to be 'integrity', 'teamwork' and 'professional'—or they feel like generic values statements borrowed from other companies' websites or picked out of an MBA handbook, then it might be time for a review and refresh.

Keen to revisit the organisation's values but not sure where to start? Here are some ideas.

Activity 1: Develop or review organisational values

Values should not be imposed on staff from 'higher up' or be a public relations exercise. Employees must be included in the process of choosing the organisational values and deciding what they mean to everyone's everyday work. You might choose to poll all staff, select a cross-section of people from across the business to form a committee or run a values brainstorming workshop. If organisational values already exist, you can either start with blank paper and create new values from scratch, or review and revise the existing values.

TEAM ACTIVITY
Values brainstorming workshop

1. Together, brainstorm what everyone in the team considers to be the values that the organisation aspires to. Have staff call out their ideas, explaining what they mean if unclear, and write them all on a whiteboard. Don't stop until all the possibilities have been exhausted—it should fill the board!

2. Get everyone to come up to the board and individually place a sticker or dot next to the top five values that most resonate with them, guide their everyday work and inspire them.

3. Identify the 10 most popular values. Some similar values may have both received some votes (such as kindness and compassion, or competitiveness and ambitious), which together would make that value a contender.
   Discuss with the team where there is overlap and how they might be merged.

4. This activity can be done by teams across the organisation, in workable focus groups of up to 25 people. After all the

(continued)

183

TEAM ACTIVITY
Values brainstorming workshop (*cont'd*)

groups have met, review the results. It's likely that the top 10 values from each focus group will be very similar. The most commonly preferred values identified in these brainstorming workshops will form a shortlist, then a representative staff group or the leadership team can confirm the most preferred values for the organisation.

Activity 2: HR or team managers explore what the values really mean

Even when the values have been agreed on across the organisation, some employees will feel particular resonance with some values and not relate so well to others. That's natural. Having regular discussions with your team about the organisation's values, and what they mean for us in practice, ensures that everyone understands the organisation's expectations and that the culture is heading in the right direction. Over time, your team members will form their own understanding of what the values mean and may put their own spin or emphasis on them.

TEAM ACTIVITY
Define the organisational values

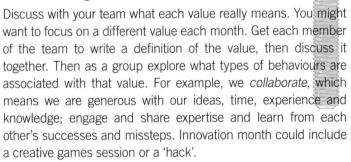

Discuss with your team what each value really means. You might want to focus on a different value each month. Get each member of the team to write a definition of the value, then discuss it together. Then as a group explore what types of behaviours are associated with that value. For example, we *collaborate*, which means we are generous with our ideas, time, experience and knowledge; engage and share expertise and learn from each other's successes and missteps. Innovation month could include a creative games session or a 'hack'.

Activity 3: HR and senior managers promulgate the values

Human Resources and senior managers can make sure that the values don't simply exist on a faded poster or a fridge magnet somewhere in the workplace. You can make sure that the values are real, consistent across the organisation's other written statements of expectations and front-of-mind for all staff.

Conduct a *mini-audit of employment contracts, policies and procedures,* to see whether they are consistent with the values and whether they are leading to the right outcomes. Like the 'Check yourself' review of unconscious bias affecting decision making (page 176) and 'Check your systems and processes' (page 175), think through the rules and guides to decision making, and whether they are privileging the right values (flexibility vs strictness? collaboration vs competition?).

You could also make *short videos* of staff members talking about a time when they lived (or saw someone else live) the organisation's values, and circulate them to everyone via email.

Give away a *fun reminder* of the organisation's values such as a drink bottle, lanyard, 'thank you' postcards or notepads.

Activity 4: Managers of teams bring the values to life

Okay, your organisation has values. Excellent. But are they lived and breathed by your team every day? Do they resonate in your team's culture? Are the values raised as you work through difficult decisions, apply policies and make judgements? There are many ways to incorporate the organisation's values into our day-to-day work and make them more real for the team. The frontline supervisor can make the organisational values relevant for the team from day to day, and translate the values into real behavioural expectations.

When *making difficult decisions together,* consider the options in light of the organisation's values. Recognising that the tricky decisions are often in the 'grey area' of ethics —where there is no 'right' and 'wrong' answers—be true to the values, even if the decision will be unpopular or inconsistent with industry trends.

Use team meetings to review and debrief successes and failures, remembering that every decision and every response made either affirms or chips away at our values. Was what happened a good example of one of the organisation's core values at work? Did we compromise our values in any way?

Refer to your organisation's values in *internal and external correspondence,* and in email footers.

Each week, ask a team member to *discuss one of the values in a team meeting.* What does it mean to them? What kinds of behaviours do they associate with that value? Can they share any examples they have seen of that value being 'lived and breathed' in the workplace?

TOOL #10
BUILD A CULTURE OF FEEDBACK

A team doesn't become dysfunctional overnight. Little things often go wrong within teams—missed deadlines, snide remarks, unfair decisions. A dysfunctional team is created when those 'little things' keep on happening and become entrenched as part of the team's culture.

Part of rebuilding a team's functioning is to make sure that problems that arise in the future will be raised, early and in a safe environment, by the employee who has a concern, so problems can be handled promptly. When the team culture encourages the sharing of concerns, complaints and feedback—including ideas for innovation and improvement—this affirms to employees that the organisation doesn't want the team to revert to dysfunctional operation, and that the employees' experience of the workplace is valued.

This is a key element of holding everyone accountable to the same standard of conduct. It will make it less likely that the unethical conduct of a Bad Apple, gossip, toxic personality or discriminatory decision maker will go undetected.

The benefits of encouraging feedback and enabling complaints

Silence (or a lack of complaints and feedback) is not necessarily golden. Failing to support employees to raise their concerns puts your organisation at greater risk of fraud and other misconduct. Typical organisations lose 5 per cent of their annual revenues to fraud, and tip-offs from employees are consistently and by far the most common method of detection. In organisations with external complaints hotlines for employees, the fraud they do experience is 41 per cent less costly and is detected 50 per cent more quickly.

Avenues of feedback and complaint enable HR, managers and leaders to learn about conflict, trouble spots and risks *before* employees depart, make compensation claims for stress, call lawyers and unions, or start complaining to customers. (How many of us have stood in line in a retail store, waiting for a fitting room to be available, and had to listen to two customer service employees complain to each other about shift rosters or favouritism?)

Crucially, by hearing about problems and concerns early on, you can respond early and effectively to misconduct before it escalates, and minimise: negative impacts on the health and wellbeing of employees; legal liability for wrongdoing; external complaints to regulators, unions and courts; and poor publicity, including on social media.

Remember, hearing about a problem does not mean the problem has just been created; it was there already, bubbling away under the surface. If an employee brings a problem to your attention, they have gifted you with the opportunity to address it before it causes more damage. Would you rather wait for customer complaints, declining sales and nasty public comments on social media?

Barriers to open and honest feedback

While statistics vary, most studies report that around one in five people who witness or experience wrongdoing or misconduct in their organisation will make a formal complaint about it. There are many reasons why employees don't raise concerns about questionable (or downright unethical) things they see in the workplace, including not knowing how to do so; fear of retribution (losing their job, damaged relationships, reputational damage); a belief that 'it is not my responsibility—someone else can handle it'; perceptions that managers are involved in the wrongdoing, will not respond constructively or will take the feedback personally; fear that the effort involved in complaining will be pointless, as it will not result in any change; a perception (whether accurate or not) that a previous complaint was brushed under the carpet, poorly managed or ignored; or fear of 'sticking their neck out' and being seen as part of the problem.

Building a feedback culture

Here are some things managers can do to encourage staff to speak their mind.

1. Seek feedback—don't wait for it!

Keeping an open door is a great start, but don't wait for people to come to you. Go out and ask them about their experiences. Set aside a few minutes at the end of one-on-one meetings to ask how the employee is travelling, if they have any ideas for improvement in the team or if there are any issues you should be aware of. Take team members out for coffee or lunch, and pay close attention to what they tell you. When they give you feedback, don't get defensive. Thank them for their feedback and explore it further if you need help to understand it. Reflect on the feedback, and demonstrate to the employee that you have done so.

2. Seek a skip-level meeting

In a skip-level meeting, a senior manager meets one-on-one with employees two levels below them in the hierarchy. This can be a great way for executives to stay in touch with the day-to-day realities of the business. It increases the flow of information and permits those with concerns about their manager to express those concerns to someone more senior who may be able to assist.

Similarly, a senior manager can set up a cross-level mentoring relationship, in which they seek a mentor from someone significantly less senior than they are in the hierarchy.

3. Support and protect employees who make complaints

A complainant who is victimised or leaves the organisation disenchanted by the complaints process can set the confidence and culture of your team back years. When a complaint is made, take active steps to ensure the complainant is not victimised or treated unfavourably because they have raised a complaint.

4. Make feedback conversations routine

Work to create a culture in which employees feel a sense of ownership of improvement and change initiatives, and want to be part of the solution of any wrongdoing they observe. They need to believe that speaking up, admitting mistakes, addressing concerns and exploring new ideas are a collective responsibility.

For example, include in your team meetings a regular agenda item to air problems. Describe it in positive terms, such as 'Innovations and improvements: How can we do better?' As employees bring up issues and concerns (either that they have observed, or on behalf of the team), discuss them without defensiveness, blame or retribution against the employee who raised them. This will normalise negative feedback, and increase the general sense of safety and trust.

5. Enable bystanders to act

Observers of occupational violence, workplace bullying, harassment and discrimination are often paralysed by 'the bystander effect': when a person needs help, most bystanders are reluctant to intervene and simply stand by without assisting. The more observers there are, the less the likelihood of any one person intervening, because they believe someone else will or should intervene.

'Upstanders' or whistleblowers can play a crucial role in the dynamics of workplace misconduct, because they have the power to end it by standing up to the perpetrator or reporting it to management. Bullies, in particular, are cowards and when confronted they are likely to desist in the face of peer pressure.

Encourage your team to speak up when they observe poor treatment of colleagues, to support the victim, to make it clear to other colleagues they won't be involved in gossip or harassing behaviour, and to intervene directly if they observe unacceptable behaviour. It's crucial that the supervisor role-models being a good upstander. Always call out bad behaviour, even when the culprit is someone more senior.

Remember, bystanders will only have confidence to intervene or report bad behaviour if they have confidence that the organisation takes such reports seriously and deals with them effectively and fairly. If a previous upstander was victimised or made redundant, or if the employer is clearly turning a blind eye to collateral damage caused by a powerful employee, they will not intervene or report.

6. Conduct exit interviews

Exit interviews of departing employees can be a treasure trove of information. Granted, the exiting employee may not give you a report of the average experience of the remaining workforce, given they are either leaving for good reasons (retiring or moving on to a better position) or bad (termination or redundancy). However, it's likely they will feel they can tell you things they would not have shared while still employed, even if they phrase observations carefully in order to avoid burning bridges. Use the opportunity to find out the real reasons that employees are leaving. Ask them open-ended questions such as, 'If there were three things you could change about what you experienced as an employee here, what would they be?'

7. Know how to respond to complaints

As a manager, your first interaction with a team member who has a complaint or negative feedback is crucial. It can dictate how the individual, and ultimately the whole team, feels about the complaints process, and your openness to improvements. Remember the following aspects of your role in the complaints process:

- Explain the complaints process, and apply the process consistently (don't state you are applying a process then deviate from it).

- Listen, treat the complainant fairly and with empathy, and seek to understand their concerns.

- Actively explore what is really going on, and determine if the employee is just venting or raising a serious issue that requires resolution.

- Identify any low-level, systemic issues that could develop into a bullying or sexualised culture.

- Determine whether urgent action (formal complaint or serious conflict) or progressive action (culture change) is required.

- Consider if you need help to unpack the issues and assess the risks, before you develop a strategy to respond.

- Understand your responsibility (if any) to personally address the complaint.

- Remember, each complaint is an opportunity for you to address concerns early and demonstrate to your team that feedback is welcomed and valued.

Chapter 18

THE FIX
DEVELOP LEADERSHIP AND MANAGEMENT

STRENGTHEN THE MANAGER'S ABILITY TO GUIDE THE TEAM AND KEEP THEM ON TRACK.

If, as a manager or leader, you identified some potential gaps in your own management and leadership skills or approach, this section will help you to address them, including options for free professional development.

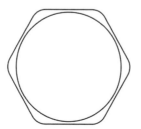
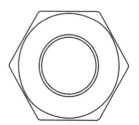

Congratulations, managers! You have recognised that in order to Fix Your Team, you need to do some work on yourself. You've proven that you have the humility, insight and integrity needed to lead your team to better functioning.

Whether or not you have decided that 'It's not the team, it's you!' (chapter 9), the fact is that unless you have only just inherited a dysfunctional team, if your team is dysfunctional *you have contributed to creating that dysfunction or allowing it to continue.* 'No!' you cry. 'There is a toxic personality in this team who has been working against me like a pack of termites!' *It was your job to identify and combat that behaviour.* 'It's not my fault that Juan and Peter in my team had an affair!' you protest. 'I've reminded them of the conflict-of-interest policy—that should have been enough!' *Creating active interventions to keep Juan and Peter working constructively, and managing gossip and innuendo that was still going three months later, was your responsibility.* 'The skeleton in the closet happened on someone else's watch!' you complain. 'The team will get over it eventually.' *They are looking to you to address the grief and the silos, and no one else can do it for them.*

In chapter 13, 'Where to start', we suggest that before you start to Fix Your Team, you might need to gather some more information and explore to what extent you are in fact part of the problem. Perhaps you conducted a workplace review, 360-degree feedback on your own management, or employee survey, and you learned some things about yourself, or about how others perceive you (which can be just as important).

The anonymous comments of your managers, your co-workers and the people who report to you may, for example, have highlighted your tendency to avoid conflict. It helped, reading this, that people also praised you for your strong work ethic and your technical prowess, but the survey has forced you to look squarely at your tendency to avoid the hard conversations that are needed to keep a workplace functioning well. Perhaps you know deep down that you avoid opportunities to nip any performance issues in the bud with particular team members, dreading the upset you might cause. You hate doing annual performance reviews: in fact, you give everyone more or less the same benign feedback and generous scores, so you can get them over and done with quickly.

You may also have had an opportunity to reflect on certain factors that influence how you behave at work, which is discussed in chapter 2, 'Unprofessional conduct'. Maybe you have had a few 'aha' moments. You may have realised, for example, that you tend to avoid conflict in all aspects of your life. That might not be so surprising, if you come from a family where one parent was needlessly aggressive and the other withdrawn and sad. Fully appreciating the flaws in both these approaches to life, and determined to avoid falling into the patterns of either parent, you would like to adopt braver and more purposeful behaviours.

The other important insight you've likely had is that you got your job because of hard work and skills that were well developed for the technical tasks at hand. Perhaps you have never been trained or properly prepared for the challenges of managing difficult people or dealing with the conflicts and problems that inevitably arise in the workplace. Maybe you didn't have the time or resources to access training in the fine arts of communication, delegation, performance and risk management, or you weren't given the freedom or empowerment to exercise those skills.

What can you do to make yourself even stronger and more sophisticated in the leadership role you hold?

TOOL #11
TRAIN THE MANAGER

Managers, reflect on the feedback you have just received from your team, your peers and your own supervisor. What managerial skills have you decided you want to build? Here are some skills that managers commonly wish to practise.

1. Managing conflict

Reflection questions: Are there any employee situations that I struggle to deal with calmly and effectively? When employees disagree with each other and the discussion becomes aggressive or blaming, do I know how to intervene?

Conflict in the workplace is inevitable. There will always be disagreements about workplace matters and personality clashes. Healthy disagreement over the way forward and new ways of doing things is a vital ingredient of a competitive and innovative workplace. Conversely, conflict that involves personal insults, bitterness, negativity and repeated rounds of bitchiness is damaging and unhelpful. Left unresolved, such conflict can intensify and spread, affecting more than the two initial antagonists.

As a manager, you need to learn how to address unconstructive conflict promptly and thoroughly, and its underlying causes, how your own experiences with conflict affect your responses, and what to do when you hear allegations of misconduct.

There are some great resources for self-guided learning about managing conflict. *It's All Your Fault at Work* (2015) by Bill Eddy is a good place to start, if you want to build your skills in dealing with colleagues with high-conflict behaviours. To explore the motivations beneath behaviours you are witnessing, and whether you are unwittingly sabotaging the effectiveness of your own efforts, read *Leadership and Self-Deception* (2004) by the Arbinger Institute.

2. Being present

Reflection questions: Do I actively enable my employees to be the best they can be, or do I leave them alone and apply more of a 'sink or swim' approach? If I think I am truly available to my employees, how do I demonstrate this to them?

A common complaint we hear from teams is that their manager is 'not available'. This might be because they are out seeing customers, dealing with other functions in the business or delivering their own projects. Often they are physically present but not really engaged with the team. Even where the manager believes they have an open-door policy, in reality, staff sometimes feel that the manager is not accessible or doesn't listen.

How much of your working day is spent really engaging, communicating and connecting with your employees? To demonstrate genuine interest in how they are travelling, it's not enough to tell them they can come to you anytime, and to meet with them once a year for a formal performance development chat.

Give some thought to arranging routine catch-ups with no particular agenda, so you can be sure you've made time to listen. Being visible can also be achieved by walking through the site or office every day, once most people have arrived, so they literally *see you*. Pausing to chat to staff makes you available, in case there's anything on their minds.

To help explore mindfulness at work, respected teacher Thich Nhat Hanh wrote *Work* (2012). You can explore further how to be fully present for your team, your family and yourself in Susan Smalley and Diana Winston's *Fully Present* (2010). There are also some classic texts on being deliberate in how you spend your time each day, such as Peter Drucker's *The Effective Executive* (2011).

3. Walk the talk: values

Reflection questions: *When I am tested or put under real pressure, am I demonstrating moral courage and being true to the organisation's values? Are there any bad habits or 'below the line' behaviours to which I fall prey when I am under stress?*

What if, in a 360-degree review, your team delivers the unmistakable message that you are failing to live your organisation's values? This is a pretty confronting message, but try to see it as an opportunity to reflect.

Would you be proud of how you treat all your employees, if the worst of your behaviour was reported in the media? If there was footage from a hidden 'nanny cam' or smartphone in your office that recorded how you speak to your employees when you are up against a deadline, would you be proud of how you conducted yourself? If you received an anonymous complaint, addressed to you personally, against one of your peers, would you have the moral courage to act?

Take a moment to examine your organisation's values. Walking the talk means you live the values of the organisation, make sound decisions and act fairly. Walking the talk means you have *integrity*, even when under pressure.

Thinking about ethics isn't just 'nice' – it makes good business sense. There is a strong case for values-driven management, demonstrated in academic research: *Leadership, Culture and Management Practices of High Performing Workplaces in Australia* (2011) by Dr Christina Boedker and others. You can learn more about ethical leadership in *Managing by Values* (2003) by Ken Blanchard and Michael O'Connor, and also *Authentic Leadership* (2017) published by Harvard Business Review.

4. Having difficult conversations

Reflection questions: What conversation do I know, deep down, I should be having at work? Why have I been putting it off? How can I develop the skills and confidence now to have that conversation?

Every manager has to have difficult conversations in any number of roles, including as the judge of performance standards, the granter of annual leave applications and the overseer of project completion. Managers often have to deliver bad news and criticism, determine the sharing of resources, ask tricky questions and handle delicate situations, which often involve the intersection of employees' personal lives, career ambitions and daily experiences.

Right now, identify a work conversation that you have been avoiding and that you know you should have, and practise following the process set out in Tool #1. Keep practising! Having difficult conversations will never feel easy but, as you become more skilled, it will feel less awkward and risky.

In addition to Tool #1 of *Fix Your Team*, 'Train everyone to have important conversations', we recommend Susan Scott's *Fierce Conversations* (2004) if you'd like to develop your skills in this area.

5. Ensuring clarity

Reflection questions: Why does my team appear confused about what they, as individuals and as a team, are responsible for achieving? Why do we seem to have the same conversations over and over again, with no progress?

The manager's role in ensuring all team members have clarity in relation to their role, responsibilities, deadlines and standards, and in holding people accountable to achieve those standards, is so important that it gets its own chapter in this book: Tool #12, 'Ensure clarity—Hold people accountable!'. For an even deeper dive into holding people accountable for achievement, you can also read Susan Scott's *Fierce Leadership* (2011) and Kerry Patterson's *Crucial Accountability* (2013).

Professional self-development on a shoestring

Having recognised the need for you to hone and practise certain management skills, you have a few options for training and development activities, even if you have little or no budget for it.

You can access the *free, downloadable resources* at www. fix-your-team.com. At this site you can also subscribe to Worklogic's weekly blog and listen to our podcasts and webinars on demand (including a series of webinars on the five topics in this Tool), to learn more about building a healthy workplace culture and addressing hotspots of poor conduct.

Conduct research online and ask people whose opinions you value about what *high-quality training courses* are available that will address those skill gaps you have now identified. Approach your supervisor to find out whether any financial support is available for you to attend these courses. Be specific about the studies that will be of most benefit to you. Even if there is no financial support available through your organisation, in Australia such courses will often be tax deductible (and will always be career-building) if you pay for them yourself.

Also check out *MOOC platforms* (massive open online courses) such as Coursera, edX and FutureLearn. Most of these courses are of high quality, free of charge and offered by some of the world's best universities. Completed online, they can all be done in the privacy of your office or home, or even on the train during your daily commute.

There's nothing like learning from someone who has done it before. Approach someone in management whom you respect—they do not need to be with your organisation, although that would probably be easiest—and ask them if they would *mentor* you. Explain your plan for self-guided professional development with specific areas of focus, and ask if they would be your coach and sounding board. Seek their agreement to work through challenges as they arise, particularly problems in the team that you are actively addressing.

Consider being *honest and open* with your team about your plan for professional development. For some people, this is the hardest step to take, but—trust us—it is the most rewarding and relationship building! It demonstrates humility, respect and openness to feedback.

Once you have identified and reflected on your skill gaps as a manager, and have mapped out a plan of action endorsed by the organisation, ask your team for their help. Share your insights, encourage them to discuss openly their experience of being managed by you, and outline your plans for improvement. Ask them, genuinely, to help you get better at your leadership role. Ask them to remind you of your undertakings if you start to slip.

Intrinsic to this approach is your acknowledgement that everyone you work with has some agency in creating a better working environment, as well as their own incentive for improving things. Inviting your colleagues to help make you the most effective you can be in leading the team, and make everyone's time at work more fruitful and positive, is truly empowering for everyone.

TOOL #12
ENSURE CLARITY—HOLD PEOPLE ACCOUNTABLE!

Why does my team appear confused about what they, as individuals and as a team, are responsible for achieving? Why do we seem to have the same conversations over and over again, with no progress? If these reflection questions are familiar to you, as the team's manager, then you need to work on your ability to set clear roles, responsibilities, deadlines, and standards of conduct and performance for every member of your team. You need to create clarity. You also need to get better at holding people accountable for achieving those responsibilities and standards.

Clarity

Clarity is about far more than a person's job description and giving them processes to follow. It's about setting clear tasks and goals that are Specific, Measurable, Achievable, Reasonable and Time-bound (SMART). It also includes the organisation's expectations about how employees are supposed to interact with others in the workplace.

The employee needs to know who is a stakeholder in the achievement of their work. (We mentioned in chapter 11 our pet peeve about dotted-line reporting! Everyone must have a 'line manager', not a 'dotted line manager', 'fuzzy manager' or 'depends-who-is-around manager'.)

Clarity about the day-to-day work the employee has been contracted to achieve is vital. It requires giving good direction when delegating a task—including all the information the person needs in order to complete the task, some guidance about how to approach it, and an understanding of what you are expecting as the end result. This is particularly important if the task isn't something the team member has completed before. Failure to do so can lead to disappointment and frustration on both sides, as we see in the following case study.

CASE STUDY
CLARITY AFTER THE FACTS

Peter, a senior manager with years of banking experience, is a confident operator. Advising big corporate clients is his sweet spot. He has a strong reputation in the industry, but he is finding it increasingly hard to identify good associates in the bank who will work with him, and that is starting to limit the size of the deals he can work on. He has access to big clients, and associates want exposure to that type of work, but people tend to work with Peter for a few months then transfer elsewhere.

Today he needs to give some honest, direct feedback to Tran. Seen as a 'wunderkind', Tran is bright and has risen fast in the bank. Tran has been working with Peter on negotiating a new debt facility with a large auto parts company. Peter feels that Tran's work on a debt contract has missed the mark.

Tran is sitting across from Peter in his office. 'Look Tran,' says Peter, 'the borrower's warranties are just not sufficient. They don't cover accuracy of their financial position, and the definition of Events of Default is too limited.' Looking a little defensive, Tran replies, 'These are standard terms.' 'Not for a deal of this size', counters Peter. 'Our risk isn't sufficiently covered. Where was Legal on this?' 'Legal wasn't involved. You said to draw it up myself, so we get it to the customer this week', says Tran.

Peter is starting to get frustrated, which is showing in his snide and biting tone. 'For a deal worth this much I'm surprised you didn't get Legal's input if you were struggling, Tran. I expected

---

> more of you.' Tran is the one to look angry now. 'I didn't *struggle*. I did what you told me to do. I've brought you the draft. If you'd wanted something different, you should have made that clear. Both of us have wasted time on this now.' Peter's eyes narrow. 'Leave it with me, Tran. It's clear to me that if I want it done properly, I have to do it myself. That will be all.' Tran leaves Peter's office and immediately emails his buddy associates: *You were right about Peter. What a brute.*

You will not be able to hold a member of staff accountable for the achievement of something, unless you were *both* crystal clear, upfront, about what was supposed to be achieved by when and to what standard. If the manager is not sure quite what they wanted to begin with, they can't expect to feel anything but disappointment at the outcome. The employee will inevitably deliver something that is not quite right. An ambiguous goal is a sure-fire cause of frustration!

When you are delegating to an employee, the employee will want to appear as though they understand what you are asking them to do. They may even *believe* they understand. Test this! Ask the employee to describe in their own words what they are setting out to achieve, and how they intend to go about that. Offer guidance and support, and let them know you'll check back in to see how they are going.

Accountability

Much of the challenge that managers face in building a culture of accountability is how they successfully prioritise their oversight of employees' work. Managers who have a laissez-faire style must apply a different approach, which may feel foreign to them, if they are managing a dysfunctional team.

Don't let the little things slide when it comes to *professional conduct* in the workplace, *compliance* with regulations that gives your organisation its 'licence to operate', and how the team members live the *values*. When it comes to values and compliance, the little things *are* the culture. The manager needs to know what they expect of the team, and what the team members should expect of each other, to communicate those expectations and to be strict about upholding them.

For the employees' *performance of tasks*, you can use a somewhat looser and more flexible approach, as you gain confidence and as you get to know how every member of your team approaches their work. Each one will have their own working style. Perhaps some apply a burst of energy at the last minute, the night before the client presentation. Others will want to talk through with you, at length and in detail, all the risks of each task within their role. Some will dislike authority and want to be free agents, reticent to share any details unless they really need your help or approval. Others will need little guidance, but it will matter to them that you are aware of their workload and the details of their work, so they feel cared about.

TIP FOR MANAGERS
Avoid micromanagement

Apply careful judgement in how you direct your attention and when you correct people. Trying to watch every act, oversee every task and observe every lunchroom conversation in real time will leave the manager exhausted, and the team feeling micromanaged and grumpy!

After delegating a task, don't wait for the employee to come back to you if they need clarification or help. Most people are proud and prefer to appear independent. Instead, suggest you meet with the employee again soon to discuss how the project is progressing, and send them a calendar invitation. The employee may want to fob you off and appear self-sufficient, but it's part of your role to support them to achieve the work.

Don't ignore your own gut feeling if you lack confidence in their likely achievement. Even if someone tells you 'it's all fine here', don't be afraid to test that. Rather than ask, 'Is it all on track for Friday?', for example, be more specific and ask open-ended questions like, 'How would you describe the quality of the data you've received from the customer?' or 'What extra input would make you even more confident that we're on track?' You can also test the extent to which they have managed risks: 'In case I get pulled onto the ABC audit on Friday morning, how much time do you think I'll need to review the report? I'm aware that it's due by close of business.' Delve into the reality of the situation, rather than accepting platitudes.

If a task appears to be going off the rails, *do not jump in to complete the task for your employee*. It is very tempting to 'save' an employee who is failing to hold up their end of the bargain. If you make the decision they are accountable to make, finish off work they started or get a customer relationship back on track, you not only let them off the hook for their inadequate performance, but also give them an excuse for repeated failure in future. You must give your staff the chance to learn from their mistakes (without letting them hang themselves).

If someone fails to deliver, don't jump down their throats with accusations. Seek an explanation, and guide them to understand the impact their failure to keep their word will have on others. Doing this, without blaming or labouring the point, will help them to understand your disappointment and the real importance of the standard you set. Maybe their failure increased the workload of the team to get the project delivered. Maybe people will be less likely to trust them in future. Maybe their colleagues will start to resent them, because this has happened too many times.

Welcome mistakes as opportunities for development and learning, rather than for blaming. Keep in mind there may be something else going on for that person that you don't know about. Perhaps they are struggling with a personal crisis (chapter 4) or overdoing a task out of insecurity. No matter what the reason for their failure, almost everyone can learn. As a wise boss of ours once said, 'Only Allah is perfect'.

Everyone feels uncomfortable when having difficult conversations like this. It can feel patronising and awkward, and you may resent that you need to have this conversation in the first place (What a waste of my time! I shouldn't have to be pointing out such obvious things!). It can feel uncomfortable to demand the best that a person can bring to the job, and to call them on it when they fail to deliver, but remember this is part of your job. By holding your team accountable, everyone—even the employee who has failed—will be better off.

The culture of accountability that you are building will soon become strong enough to be a force of its own, and will therefore take less effort by you to maintain. The team will learn that you do pay attention, and do judge whether they achieve the things they are accountable to achieve and they will require less day-to-day oversight. In this way, as you gain traction in building a culture of accountability, you'll learn when to be 'loose' about your supervision and direction of staff, and when to be 'tight'.

One final suggestion: don't forget to celebrate success and be grateful for achievement when things go well! Seize opportunities to celebrate success, to affirm the standards you have set, to reward people for competency and to find more joy in the everyday.

Chapter 19

THE FIX
CARE FOR EACH OTHER

OFFER FLEXIBILITY, SUPPORT AND CARE IN TOUGH TIMES.

The Tools in this section will provide you with some practical and constructive ideas about how you can care for and support the team when it is grappling with difficult emotional challenges or has experienced recent trauma.

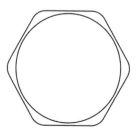
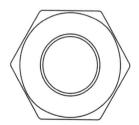

TOOL #13
SUPPORT THE TEAM THROUGH
PERSONAL CRISES AND CHALLENGES

Managing an employee who is dealing with a personal crisis (chapter 4) can be extremely challenging for any manager. Many managers can be reluctant to enter into discussions with employees about personal issues—unsure how to begin, embarrassed by the subject matter or nervous about breaching the employee's privacy.

The truth is that, as a society, the line between our personal and work lives is rapidly diminishing. Flexible work practices and the ubiquity of technology mean that our personal and work lives increasingly overlap.

Thankfully, most personal crises will require support for only a temporary period before things return to normal. It's important to remember that your role as a manager is not to advise employees on how to deal with the particular issue they are facing. Rather, focus on providing them with the support they need to address the issue, while still enabling the rest of your team to function as efficiently as possible.

Approaching the person with compassion and kindness will go a long way to helping them through a difficult time, and sends an important message to other employees that you value and support your team.

The manager's role

As a manager, you face the triple challenge of finding the best way to support a team member while also balancing the needs of the rest of the team and getting the job done.

You may be conscious that one team member's reduced capacity, unusual behaviour or unplanned absences are affecting the workload and morale of the whole team.

This is a complex area where, for a manager, multiple responsibilities can intersect. For ethical and legal reasons, you must work with the struggling team member constructively, fairly and with compassion. It is *illegal to discriminate* against anyone in the workplace because of a disability; this includes mental illness and psychological disorders, physical disability and any side effects of medical treatment.

Your active support of a member of your team who is experiencing a personal crisis will have a huge impact on their experience and ability to move forward. The team member's *recovery* is undoubtedly a major priority for them; it should be for their colleagues and employer too. Supporting a worker with activity-based rehabilitation and their return to suitable work has been proven to improve general health and reduce psychological distress.

You will, of course, need to talk in depth with the affected person about the support they need and the range of options that might assist them to stay connected until the crisis passes.

Despite this, your team member's *performance* may continue to deteriorate, or their behaviour may be so erratic and extreme that it causes a risk to the *workplace health and safety* of other members of the team or of clients. If their personal crisis or illness is damaging their ability to perform their job to an acceptable standard, or causing an unsatisfactory risk to health or safety, you may need to performance manage them. If they cannot improve their performance, you will ultimately need to make a decision about whether they have the ability to fulfil the *inherent requirements of the role*. To do this, you may need advice and opinions from the struggling team member's treating doctors, as well as legal advice.

Most personal crises do pass. If they are handled well, your team will emerge stronger, wiser and richer for having extended itself to look after the person, who, as many of us know, might next be you or me.

Seven things you can do to assist a team member going through a personal crisis

A personal crisis is just that—personal. There is no 'one size fits all' approach. Some people may require extra leave; others may find respite by staying at work through a difficult personal time. Exploring flexible options is key.

1. Ask them what they need

If you are aware that a team member is going through a challenging personal time, ask them privately what support they need. You don't need to know the specific details of the crisis; you just need to identify what you can do to support them.

Supporting a team member through a difficult time might require the manager to deal differently with different people. It is possible to treat people differently and still be fair to all. Where appropriate, explain the basis for your actions to the team.

2. Make a plan

Once you understand what that team member needs, confirm what your support plan will be. Identify what work will be done, and by whom, for the relevant period, and any time off required. Don't plan ahead beyond the next month, as the situation may change, and be clear that the plan can be revised accordingly.

If the employee needs work to be reallocated, do involve other employees in discussions too.

3. Consider reasonable adjustments

Australian legislation requires that employers adequately consider reasonable adjustments in the workplace for workers with illness or injury. A 'reasonable adjustment' is making changes to a job—including modified duties, working hours, locations, job rotation, modifying equipment and other factors—so the worker can perform the genuine and reasonable requirements of the job. They should be specific to the employee's needs and be regularly reviewed over time. The Australian Human Rights Commission's *Workers with Mental Illness: a Practical Guide for Managers* (2010) includes some excellent guidance.

For someone who is experiencing depression, a reasonable adjustment might be, for instance, to offer a later start in the morning. For someone experiencing a relationship breakdown during which they must assume sole custody of children, reducing hours so childcare can be managed could be considered. Remember to write these arrangements into a plan. Of course, once people are well again and the crisis has passed, the conditions applicable to all team members should resume (noting that these conditions might include degrees of flexibility).

One of the most practical ways you can support someone going through a personal crisis is to give them flexibility around the way they work: flexible hours, including starting late or early, compressed working days or working from home, attending meetings via Skype or conference call, or flexibility around time off, including personal leave, unpaid leave or extra holiday leave.

Consider whether you can change the 'weight' of their work. For instance, is there a particular time-sensitive or stressful aspect of their job that you could reallocate or suspend temporarily?

4. Check in regularly

Once you have agreed on a plan, check in regularly with your team member to see how they are travelling and consider any further adjustments to the plan over time. Encourage them to stay in touch with you. Don't assume they are alright because you haven't heard from them.

5. Communicate with and support the rest of your team

As discussed in chapter 4, the impact of a team member dealing with a personal crisis may be felt by other team members. They may be providing emotional support or shouldering a greater workload to cover their colleague's incapacity. It is important to communicate to the other members of the team any changes to working arrangements that affect them, while also respecting the privacy of the employee being accommodated. For members of the team who may be emotionally upset by the crisis that their colleague is experiencing, remind them that counselling or the Employee Assistance Program is available.

Privacy is important: check first with the team member before sharing details of their situation. If they are uncomfortable with sharing private information, you can simply advise other employees that their colleague needs some time to deal with some private issues and explain the interim changes to working arrangements.

6. Use training judiciously

This might be the right time to foster and re-emphasise the need for tolerance and compassion in your team. Misconduct such as bullying and gossip can flourish where communication is restricted, as it is (justifiably) when personal privacy is an issue. Misunderstandings and misinterpretation of unexpected behaviour can lead to the isolation of people at just the time when they most need kindness and support.

Find out who in your area runs the best, most inspired training sessions on workplace tolerance, anti-bullying, team cohesion or the benefits of workplace diversity, and engage them to help you all keep on track.

7. Handle misconduct allegations

If the struggling team member has made a complaint against a colleague, or complaints have been made against them, handle those complaints in accordance with your organisation's policies and procedures. It is important that these are seen to be applied equitably. Keep in mind that any response to their misconduct in the workplace must be accompanied by clear offers of support, such as counselling or leave.

Remember, this situation is normal. Stressful as these episodes can be, do remind yourself they are in fact *normal.* Every one of us will experience periods in our lives when we struggle to cope, because of illness, personal crisis, bereavement or exhaustion. At those times what we need, and have a right to expect, is the genuine support, patience and accommodation of the people with whom we work.

TOOL #14
DEALING WITH OVERWORK

Remember chapter 12, on overwork? This is one of the more visible dysfunctions of a team. It's identified pretty easily, but combating the drivers of overwork is a different matter.

A culture of overwork within your team, or the organisation at large, can be daunting to change, particularly if it is a culture you have inherited. It is important that you address it, as overwork will eventually take a serious toll on your team's health and wellbeing, as well as its ethics and work quality. Here's where you should start.

Identify the extent of the problem

The first step is to assess the extent and severity of the problem. If you are not already doing so, start to monitor systematically each team member's working hours and workload for a few weeks. Identify and measure what unpaid overtime employees are working. Consider whether part-time workers are putting in more unpaid overtime than full-time workers, calculated as a percentage of their paid hours. In a culture of overwork, part-time workers often end up working almost full-time hours for part-time pay, out of an unwarranted sense of guilt.

Explore with your colleagues in Human Resources, Workplace Health and Safety, and Risk what the organisation is currently carrying in costs of absenteeism, presenteeism, sick leave and turnover. Are these trending up or down? Can you benchmark your organisation against others in the industry? How does your team compare with the rest of the organisation? Explore (on a de-identified basis) the trends in worker's compensation claims, such as any rise in psychological health concerns, and what the staff said in the last employee engagement survey about workload and exhaustion.

Can the workload change?

Think about the goals, projects or schedules your team needs to meet now, or in the next business cycle, and whether these are truly realistic. If they are not, discuss and seek support from your line manager to re-prioritise. Burnout can be a real risk to the achievement of goals (as well as an obvious risk to health, safety and wellbeing), so it is rightfully taken into account in project planning. Can anything in the team's schedule be identified as 'aspirational only' or its delivery delayed?

Managers, consider any resourcing issues that you have inherited, and explore within the business how these can be rectified.

If you get no support from managers to adjust the expectations of the team members' working hours, push harder. Consider setting out the team members' working hours over the past month in an email to HR or Risk, noting the statistics from chapter 12, and alerting them to your concerns about worker wellbeing and project risk.

It may be that part of a project has to 'fail', owing to impossible deadlines, before the need for change is acknowledged.

Combat the culture of overwork

Be an ambassador for cultural change by communicating internally the true cost to the organisation of unrealistic workload expectations. The research noted in chapter 12 is a good place to start for educating others.

Research conducted by the Australia Institute led to 'National Go Home on Time Day' in November each year to encourage workers to finish work when they are meant to. Their tips for workers include the following:

- Decide what time you are going home before you go to work.

- Identify early any tasks that may need a large time commitment, and manage expectations with your boss.

- Take a lunch break to refresh and boost productivity for the afternoon.

- Schedule activities after work: meet a friend at the gym or take the kids to the park.

- Make a commitment to go home on time once a week or once a month.

- Everyone in the team can support each other to work productively and efficiently while still maintaining healthy work–life balance.

- Invite each other out to lunch and, if possible, go outside and enjoy a walk as well.

- Encourage your colleagues to use non-work time to refresh and rejuvenate, and to enjoy their leisure time. Talk about the time you spent at your kids' sports games or visiting friends.

- Explore with the team their ideas to reduce overwork, including flexible work practices, and ideas for improving efficiency and cooperation. Consider a pilot of the feasible ideas.

If you are a manager, you can have even more impact on the culture of overwork; after all, the team members look to you for guidance on working hours. (If you are a member of the team, convince the manager to take the following steps.)

- Proactively set realistic limits for your team on the use of email, taking calls and/or doing any work outside of usual work hours.

- It's all very well to tell your team that work–life balance is a priority, but if they see you working until late at night and on the weekends, it won't mean much. Let everyone know they are not expected to be contactable outside work hours. Model real 'down time' by not sending emails outside work hours. If you feel the need to draft emails after hours (for whatever reason), don't press send until 9 am the next morning—or schedule the email to send at a later time using a time delay on your email program—so there is no implied expectation that the team will have addressed those matters before the work day starts.

- Publicly note that you reward and recognise the amount and quality of their output, not the number of hours they spend in the workplace. Talk about efficiency and balance.

- Actively and publicly address overwork as a negative phenomenon. Discourage your employees from taking work home and make it clear that promotion is not based on excessive hours.

- Take aside any outlier staff who are working excessive hours and explore with them what is driving that. Do they fear they are falling behind? Are they trying to prove something, or are they driven by insecurity? Are they confused about the real measures of success for their role? Is there a lack of clarity in priorities or desired outcomes that is making it difficult for them to prioritise? Can they determine what to *stop doing*, and do they feel supported to make that decision?

If overwork is widespread in the organisation, then like any broader workplace cultural change, commitment to any of the measures you are proposing for your team must be embraced, supported and driven by the organisation's leaders. It requires a commitment from the top: a genuine understanding of the business case for a change to an efficient, productive and healthy culture, and a clear (re)commitment to the stated positive values of the organisation.

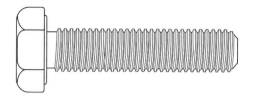

PART III
MAKING IT WORK

Managers, advisors and team members share a fundamental belief into *what they value most* about the workplace. It is how we interact with people, and how the people around us interact, that brings the most joy, inspiration, satisfaction … and the most aggravation!

In reading this book, you are acknowledging that your team is not working as it should. Take a deep breath. You know if you do nothing, the same old dysfunctions will continue to damage the productivity and happiness of your working days, and the dysfunctions may get worse. Take a deep breath and feel a sense of inner strength. Know *you can do this*, applying all you've learned in this book and all you've understood from your own experiences in the team, as well as the data and other opinions that you have gathered.

Reflect on the path that lies ahead. You have analysed the likely causes and thought about the elements in the Fix Your Team Toolkit that are most relevant and likely to work. Now you need to put together a plan, and garner the internal endorsement, support or approval of resourcing that you need to implement it.

None of this is easy. It takes courage and fortitude to fix problems, and grit to hang in there while the Tool is implemented, so you'll need to look after yourself. There will be no net gain if, in the process of Fixing Your Team, you end up depleted, disappointed or defeated. Just as you've applied logic and effort to assessing the state of your team, you need to keep an eye on your own wellbeing, effectiveness and energy.

Thankfully, there is a significant reward at the end of this process. As your team repairs, you and every team member will feel the heavy weight of dysfunction lift. The possibility of enjoying your job will return. Yes, it's possible that you will again look forward to coming to work each day! And, to the degree to which you have risen to the challenge of Fixing Your Team, you'll feel a new, well-earned sense of pride and confidence.

Chapter 20

CREATE A PROJECT PLAN

You wouldn't remedy an environmental spill, build a bridge or launch a new product without a clear project plan. Similarly, you won't be embarking on a sensitive and important effort to improve your team's functioning without some careful thinking, risk management and resource planning.

Assuming you have carefully identified the symptoms and causes of the team dysfunction, and assessed the likely impact of the proposed interventions, here are some other elements that your project plan must take into account.

WHAT HAS ALREADY BEEN TRIED?

The context in which you'll apply your Tools is important. One consideration is any attempts that have been made in the past. What have you, and others, already tried? What worked, and what didn't work? Explore this question with your predecessors and other longstanding employees who are familiar with the team.

Commonly, team dysfunction will have been considered by the organisation a few times in recent years—by the manager before you, and the one before that. If so, this issue may seem tired and intractable, or even 'impossible', from the perspective of the rest of the organisation. Human Resources may have been lumbered with the issue because no one in the past has been brave or skilled enough to handle it.

Perhaps, for example, a consultant was brought in two years ago to conduct a culture review, and everyone invested in that process, yet nothing changed for the better. This will give you an indication of the likely reception of another consultant or workplace review (even if the success of the current intervention is more likely).

There will probably be history in the group, and some sensitivity regarding what they are now prepared to participate in. The trust and confidence of the team in *any* intervention should be considered.

TIMING AND SEQUENCE OF STEPS

Fixing Your Team might require a series of steps: short-term priorities for what needs to happen immediately, and things that might be saved for the next budget cycle. For example, you might decide that the steps include mediation between two people who were involved in a misconduct investigation last year; training for the team on building diversity and inclusion in the workplace; and a review of workload and work practices to address the culture of overwork that seems to have crept in. Which do you do first? Can you do some simultaneously?

If you have identified more than one intervention that you'd like to apply, give some preliminary consideration to the best sequence. Ask yourself these questions:

- Is there an intervention that must occur first? If any urgent and formal intervention needs to happen to address an individual's problem behaviour, such as an investigation of misconduct or disciplinary action for undisputed wrongdoing, this should occur first.

- What steps can follow? How likely am I to get more than one bite of this cherry? Can I try 'A', and if it doesn't work, try 'B', or is it vital that the first intervention is successful?

- What's the risk of an intervention failing, compared with not doing it at all?

- Are there other ways this problem could be resolved? For example, could you consider the relocation of an employee who has some valuable skills but is a poor fit in their current role?

- What energy and attention does the team have to invest in learning, development and self-reflection? Think about the big commitments of time and attention that are already on the team's agenda for the next 12 months.

TIP FOR MANAGERS
Sequence the interventions with care

Here are a few golden rules about the sequencing of interventions:

- Be patient. Dysfunctional teams are often complex beasts, with longstanding issues that may not be immediately clear to you, even after talking one-on-one to the employees involved.

- Don't try to run two interventions at once, except perhaps a mediation between two warring employees during a period in which you are also running a training program for the whole team or some offline self-education by the manager.

- Give employees time to learn from one Tool before being invited to participate in another one. It is rare that more than one intervention is appropriate in the same month.

- Never run a mediation with employees who are also participating in a misconduct investigation.

- Save the team-building activities until after the team-repair activities. People usually need to work through trauma, conflict and anger before they can think about being compassionate, innovative and cooperative with one another.

USING INTERNAL RESOURCES AND DO-IT-YOURSELF

Most of the interventions in this book can be delivered by an internal service provider, particularly in larger organisations. Consider whether the team's manager, or someone in HR, Legal or Risk, has the right skills, credibility, time, competence, objectivity and impartiality to deliver the Tool. It could be more cost effective for the team's manager or someone in a service function to get some coaching or training to build those skills. Alternatively, is there someone somewhere else in the organisation who is developing these skills and could assist?

Not every internal service provider has dealt with issues like those your team is facing, nor will they understand the issues to the same extent as you or as the team members themselves will. Even if the internal provider has competence to deliver the Tool, they will also need both *perceived* impartiality (what the team members think of that manager) and *actual* impartiality (they haven't already assisted or advised one of the key players, and don't have a stake in a particular outcome). Further, the internal service department will need credibility with the team, something it may have lost because of past actions or political issues.

Consider talking with Human Resources about your plan and the options for internal and external providers. If an external provider is the best option, it may be that HR, rather than the team manager, will identify and select the external provider. The organisation may have a set of preferred suppliers. The manager may do best to couch the request as, 'This is the intervention I'd like to apply, and this is the resource in the organisation that has the expertise to decide how to execute it'.

HOW YOU WILL MEASURE SUCCESS

Once the intervention has been delivered, what will success look like? How will you judge whether it achieved what it was supposed to achieve? How quickly are you anticipating results? This will depend completely on the Tool you choose.

Your measures of success might include things like:

- the development of a new agenda for weekly team meetings, which is successfully adopted and still in use after three months

- Colleen looking happier at work (*yes, this could be a real measure of success!*)

- team members reporting to you, when you check in with them after eight weeks, that they feel clearer about their duties and know who to go to for help

- in the mediation, Milly and Finn reaching an agreement about how they will engage with each other at work, and the mediator reporting that they both are making significant efforts to understand each other's viewpoint

- after four sessions, more than half the team is attending the lunchtime yoga sessions the organisation runs each week

- staff are collaborating more effectively

- no one is working more than two hours' unpaid overtime per fortnight.

Chapter 21

BUILD A BUSINESS CASE

By this stage in your FYT project, you are very aware of the drivers behind the team dysfunction and what you are going to do to address it. Your colleagues—including those with authority whose affirmation you may need to proceed—have some catching up to do. They need to understand why the investment of time and resources is warranted.

SOCIALISE THE ISSUE FIRST

Before you formalise any request for approval and resources, *socialise the issue* with people who need to buy into the plan. Make sure your own manager knows what's coming and has had an opportunity to give their own input. They will have another level of understanding of the organisational politics, how your proposal will be heard by the powers-that-be and how to effect real change in this organisation. They may be able to add a level of sophistication as well as gravitas to your plan.

What you know about your manager will assist you to work out *how* you seek the manager's support. Is your manager someone who will need to participate in the decision to choose the Fix, so they can 'own' the decision? Is this the type of person who will want a one-page brief explaining the reasons why, with a business case? Alternatively, will an indirect and staged approach be more successful, talking with the manager about the problem over a period of time? You'll know, as someone who knows the manager and the team's recent history, how best to approach them so you are most likely to get a hearing.

Your goal is to build buy-in by having conversations with your supervisor. It might sound something like this.

Kairen: Well Tom, as you know I've had some concerns about the project team's functioning since I came in. I didn't want to be in this predicament either, but here we are. This is what I've identified: *[describes issues]*.

Tom: Yeah. I knew you were inheriting a challenge with that lot. Graham let it go for years. It was hard to make head or tail of it.

Kairen: Now it's affecting productivity *[describes how]* and morale. I'm getting worried that we could lose Liz, who as you know is one of the rising stars. We're not going to keep attracting people like her if we earn a reputation for being a toxic workplace.

Tom: Yeah. I always thought Graham should just knock their heads together or restructure and start again, but IR wouldn't go with it. Graham kept saying they would sort themselves out, that it was just a personality clash...

Kairen: We've tried giving them all general training about the Code of Conduct, but now it's more serious than that. From my perspective, I'm not seeing any improvement in conduct or performance. I'm not waiting for a stress claim before we take action. If we don't do anything, I think we are risking *[describes risks]*.

Tom: You're right. Project 30 Rock is too important to get derailed by this sort of *[expletive]*.

Kairen: I've worked through various options, and here's my sense of what we need to do. For an effective intervention we need to *[describes solution, plan, resourcing]*. I've talked with HR, but they feel they've already tried and don't have the influence anymore, or the patience. I can get some quotes from some external providers for *[intervention]*. I'm guessing it wouldn't cost more than $2000. What are your thoughts?

Tom: That sounds about right. The cost is immaterial, if you're confident it will move the needle and get Projects to stay on target. Send me a plan and I'll talk to Kym about who'll bear the cost.

Now Kairen can put a more detailed proposal to Tom, which he will almost certainly agree with, particularly as she has researched, justified and costed it well.

FINANCIAL RESOURCING

Most of the Tools we've outlined in *Fix Your Team* are free, and require only an investment of time and effort by the manager with some help from Human Resources. While time is always in short supply, there is little need for you to find financial backing to implement the Fix.

A few of the Tools we've recommended will require a financial investment by the organisation to get the team back on track. These are:

- employing an external consultant to conduct a workplace review to understand the team members' views of the dysfunction (chapter 13)

- bringing in a mediator, facilitator or conflict coach to help the team members resolve conflict (Tool #2)

- engaging an external investigator to investigate allegations of misconduct (Tool #4)
- running team-building programs such as barefoot bowls or a barista course (Tool #7)
- providing training courses and management books for the manager's professional self-development (Tool #11).

Most managers will have some financial provision for team training, and a straightforward way of accessing those funds (though it may not be in the form of a budget line item). Very few managers have a budget for unanticipated emergencies or essential fixes, such as a workplace review or a mediation. In any case, many of the Fix Your Team Tools are crucial but not 'urgent'.

Put simply, budgets don't anticipate that teams will become dysfunctional.

Of course, money from the budget becomes more and less available at certain times of the year, so there are poor and better times to ask. Judge carefully when you decide to make the push.

Whatever the budget, if the intervention is a formal or visible one, the manager will need to apply their skills of negotiation and persuasion to build the buy-in and commitment needed.

ARTICULATE THE VALUE OF FIXING YOUR TEAM

In order to gain the organisation's agreement for an unanticipated spend or the team's time out of the business (to participate in training or team-building, for example), the manager should make a case for why taking such action is a worthy investment.

If you need to seek approval to use a Fix Your Team Tool, demonstrate:

- the *actual damage and costs that the dysfunction has caused* for the organisation. Identify *all the costs* the dysfunction is causing, including lack of productivity, absenteeism, sick leave, resignations, recruitment costs, retraining and wasted management time

- the *risks that the dysfunction is creating or exacerbating* for the organisation, including the likelihood of sick leave, lost time defending industrial relations and safety cases in court, legal costs, workers' compensation claims, the intervention of external regulators and damage seeping into the broader organisational culture. It will become more likely that valued staff will choose to depart the organisation (the people the organisation can *least* afford to lose), while the less valued staff will stay on, diluting the net output of the team

- an estimate of the *likely benefits* to the organisation of your proposed intervention, when successfully applied. Explain the benefits in terms of improved productivity, greater creativity and innovation, and greater efficiency, and why the intervention is likely to have traction in this organisation

- *how low the relative cost of the intervention is,* compared with the actual costs and risks of the dysfunction.

Keep in mind that to create a burning platform for the change that you are seeking to make, you must focus on the *urgency* of action, and risk is a great place to start. A strong argument would be, for example, that this team dysfunction has created a risk of loss of our critical resource—namely, someone who has skills that would be difficult to replace, someone who is doing a task that has a degree of immediate urgency, or someone who is of high capital potential for the organisation in the long term and whose loss would be a big issue. The organisation will be sensitive to those types of risks, and more understanding of the need to implement the intervention promptly.

Point out that *the problem is likely to escalate* and is already sucking up large amounts of management time as well as distracting people from their daily work. The longer you leave the problem, the greater its impact on productivity and time-cost issues, and the more intractable it becomes.

Of course, there's also the issue of *reputational risk*. Depending on the nature of the dysfunction, high-profile cases might result, attracting unwelcome public attention. More likely, reputational damage will result from word-of-mouth, when departing employees tell other people about the dysfunction and the failure of management to do anything about it. Others then don't choose to join the organisation or patronise it, or to become its suppliers. Social media only exacerbates this risk: once anyone posts comments on the company's social media pages, or their own page, hundreds of people hear of the nepotism, sexism, gossip and toxic culture that was allowed to fester.

FRAMING YOUR CASE

The key task for the manager who has identified the dysfunction and the Tool is to *frame a case for intervention in the language that your business understands*. If your organisation is highly focused on costs, that's the lever you pull to get buy-in for your chosen intervention (the costs of the problem, the likely cost savings of the intervention). If the organisation is focused on health and safety, talk about the health risks of conflict in the workplace, the damage to employees' health and wellbeing caused by elevated stress levels, or the elevated workplace health and safety risks of a culture in which no one speaks up.

Whatever your organisation's values—in reality and (if it is any different) in its marketing and communications—they should be a core component of your request for internal support. Draw on the organisation's existing commitments to point out the importance of what you are proposing—that it 'puts safety first', or values integrity, equity and respect, for example.

When preparing a written business case, use language that is specific and fact-based, and refers to research where appropriate. Be objective and persuasive! Make the case for why doing something (your chosen Tool) is a more sensible option than doing nothing. The business case must cover the following ground:

- This is the problem I want to resolve.
- This is why it's important to resolve it (including the risks I will reduce, the benefits I will gain for the team and the organisation, and the gap between the ideal state of the team and the current reality).
- These are some of the options I see for resolving it.
- This is my preferred option, and why.
- This is what the future will look like once I have implemented my preferred option, including improvements I will make and how I will measure success.
- This is how it could be executed (timing, sequence of steps, potential providers).
- These are the resources I need (if you are ready to be specific).

For complex or costly interventions, seek out the resources available online to help you set out a business case, including how you will measure the impact of your intervention and use the learnings in broader systems of change and improvement.

Chapter 22

READY TO LAUNCH

At this point, give some thought to *who is best placed to raise the intervention with the team, and how*. Managers, if you are seen as part of the problem—if the team blames you, even partly, for causing the dysfunction or allowing it to intensify—are you the best person to introduce this intervention to the team? Or should it, rather, be raised by your own manager, or perhaps Human Resources? Even if you have diagnosed the problem and prescribed the solution, you may not be able to 'own it' without damaging its likely success.

Think also about *how the intervention/s are likely to be received by the team*. To what extent are the team members aware of the problems that are affecting the team's dysfunction? When they hear that you are arranging a team-building program, or that an external consultant is coming in to ask them about the team's culture, for example, will this be a surprise? Remember that not everyone in the team has taken the time, as you have, to work through this book and come to a deeper understanding of what is going on. Everyone will have their own perspective on who is at fault, and who is responsible for contributing to the clean-up. Think through all of their likely responses.

If someone in the team pushes back, engages in blame or refuses to cooperate in the intervention, how will you respond? An influential team member might respond with a 'shoot the messenger' approach out of fear of conflict, or argue that it is the manager's job to 'fix it' alone and unaided. If you have planned to combat a harmful power play, such as gossiping, silos or toxic personalities, you should anticipate a strong reaction. A venomous employee will attempt to undermine the intervention and engage in a personal attack on you. After all, your proposed intervention should directly target the source of their power, if it is well judged! Those who have enjoyed the power of manipulating, victim behaviour, blaming and undermining others will not want to lose that power. By anticipating their pushback, you'll position yourself carefully in advance—and lock in the support of those with *real* power in the organisation, including HR and your own supervisor—so any undermining will come to nothing.

Remember that you are trying something new and implementing a significant change. Moving the team from being dysfunctional to being cohesive, effective, productive and harmonious is a process of evolution. As the team's dynamic changes over time, you'll need to act as a sophisticated and calm observer guide and navigator.

As the Resistance fighter pilot urges in the first *Star Wars* movie, 'Stay on target!' throughout the process. You've won the support and resourcing for your plan to Fix Your Team, based on the strong business case you have developed. Don't forget the purpose of the plan, the key steps, the principles that underpin it and the constructive outcomes expected for everyone involved. Adapt and be flexible as needed to respond to the team dynamic as it shifts. Once you are underway, remind yourself of all the hard work you have done to untangle the mess your team was in. Believe that the process you have carefully planned is legitimate and fair to everyone. Have confidence in the plan and your role in delivering it.

If possible, and so long as the circumstances are still conducive to a successful intervention, stick to the plan. If something comes out of left field—such as the resignation or long-term leave of a key player, allegations of bullying or an organisation-wide change initiative—consider making changes to the plan only in consultation with others in the organisation whom you trust.

Chapter 23

BUCKLE UP! LOOK AFTER YOURSELF

Congratulations! You have taken the high road and decided to do the work needed to Fix Your Team. You will need to summon all your powers of professionalism, objectivity, composure and emotional intelligence to complete this important work.

There may well be emotional costs for you along the way. It is important that you are prepared to apply to yourself the same level of care you are about to apply to your team. When dealing with complaints, conflict and extreme emotion of others, you may be exposed to anger, suspicion, rudeness and other negative treatment. You may witness people expressing great sadness or anger. There may be challenges to your role, competence and authority; people may even deliberately manipulate facts and redirect accusations at you.

Addressing entrenched issues of dysfunction is potentially stressful for everyone concerned, and with stress comes poor behaviour. Accept that things may get worse before they get better! If addressed appropriately, using the Fix Your Team Toolkit, the poor behaviour *will end* and an improved regime of civility and team renewal will follow.

Here are four strategies that you can use to remain effective as you Fix Your Team, especially when you feel under pressure.

1. REFLECT ON YOUR EMOTIONAL STATE

Processes aimed at addressing dysfunction, conflict and complaints are very focused on the rights, experiences and input of the employees involved. Be sure to consider your own emotional response as well. As you address these matters, at times you may experience feelings of guilt, frustration, fear and stress. You will also likely have moments of joy, confidence and achievement as you notice real improvements occurring.

There is no 'right' or 'wrong' emotional response. What matters is that you are aware of your emotions, so they do not interfere with your professional and rational delivery of the Fix Your Team plan you have embarked upon.

Look after your wellbeing to ensure that, as you work through the plan, you can maintain your focus, professionalism and boundaries. If you can do this, you will be better able to make fair decisions and approach the next step in the plan with confidence and resilience.

One of the most taxing aspects of this process is that, during interviews and meetings, you must remain professional even when provoked. Managers often need to mask their own emotional reactions when they see others upset, blaming or acting in ways they consider unethical. They do this to remain impartial and rational, even when the other person is attempting to drag them into a vitriolic slanging match.

Keeping a 'poker face', especially when dealing with subject matter that you find unpleasant or that jars with your own values, can have an impact on your own emotional wellbeing. After such an encounter, be aware of your feelings, and physical and psychological reactions, as Ramona does in the following case study.

CASE STUDY
RAMONA'S REMEDY

Ramona inherited a difficult team in Customer Engineering Services six months ago. As one of the first steps in her Fix Your Team plan, Ramona is meeting with service technician Manish, during which she mentions reports she has received that he has been generating much of the negative and inaccurate gossip that is circulating in their workplace. She asks for his response, but Manish reacts with outrage, raising his voice and blaming others for the stories. 'And I can tell you another thing', he finishes. 'You've got no support around here. Everyone thinks you're an upstart and an idiot. You're just the reason that affirmative action programs and all that politically correct rubbish about women being the boss is just crap.' He storms out of her office.

Ramona has remained calm and respectful throughout the interview, giving Manish the chance to respond to each reported item on her list, just as she'd prepared before the meeting. On the inside, she feels sick at the insulting and sexist put-down she's just received. She is inclined to believe the reports of Manish's undermining and gossip—mainly because she has personally observed this poor behaviour by Manish—but she doesn't want to prejudge the situation or treat Manish unfairly.

Ramona takes handwritten notes throughout the meeting. After Manish leaves, she types up an email to her boss, recording the offensive things Manish has just said to her. She decides to send it to herself only at this stage, as a file note. She thinks that she might email it to her boss later, once she has decided with a clear head what to do next.

Recognising that she needs time to process her reactions, Ramona shuts off her computer and goes for a brisk walk outside the building, then takes 10 minutes to sit on a park bench and breathe deeply. Before returning to her desk, she goes to the bathroom and brushes her teeth, knowing that spitting is a

(continued)

241

CASE STUDY
RAMONA'S REMEDY (*cont'd*)

natural physical response to disgust. That night at home, although she still feels upset, she thoroughly enjoys the escapism of a Netflix binge.

---

2. KEEP YOUR EYE ON THE BIGGER PICTURE

Not all the possible causes of team dysfunction are generated within the team itself. Remain aware of external or more widespread factors that may be putting pressure on team behaviours. You may not be able to change those external factors, but it helps if you understand their impact.

Research suggests that high levels of conflict are particularly prevalent in workplace environments where there are high-level psychological triggers for aggression. Such triggers include role ambiguity, unfair procedures, frustrated goal achievement, micromanagement from the highest level down, unreasonable job demands, pay cuts or freezes, and other circumstances that can trigger uncivil, aggressive and abusive behaviour.

Put simply, people are more likely to behave badly when they are under stress, and there may be stressors over which you have no control.

You can't fix everything. Remain realistic about what you can achieve.

3. KEEP UP YOUR ENERGY LEVELS

Remain tuned in to your energy levels. Dealing with stressful issues can drain you intellectually and physically. This is particularly true if you are undertaking to Fix Your Team on top of your regular workload.

Experts on energy at work such as The Energy Project advise that we should stay in the 'performance zone' and the 'recharge zone' as much as possible, and should avoid the 'survival zone' and the 'burnout zone' wherever possible. If you don't spend time in the recharge zone, and you keep pushing yourself to perform, you risk burning out or living on survival instinct. You're worth more than that. No job requires self-sacrifice, and your burnout won't help your team either.

Burnout is a state of chronic stress and tiredness that leads to physical and emotional exhaustion, cynicism, detachment, and feelings of being ineffective and of lack of accomplishment. Signs of burnout should not be ignored.

Making time to recharge your energy levels is very important. Do things that relax you, and make sure you get enough sleep. To prevent or cope with the symptoms of burnout, consider:

- taking time to treat yourself, such as having a massage
- keeping a journal or diary
- maintaining a connection with thoughts and beliefs that are meaningful to you and give you hope
- watching your favourite comedy, for a good laugh
- spending time with people who make you feel good about yourself
- visiting places where you feel comfortable and relaxed
- making time to exercise and eat healthily.

If you are feeling burned out, take a complete break from fixing the team. Tell yourself, for example, 'I will not work on this until Wednesday morning'. Ideally, take a day off. Discuss your feelings of burnout with your supervisor if you feel comfortable doing so.

Over time, if you still find yourself feeling burned out from managing conflict and complaints, seek help from a counsellor or coach. You may be giving the same advice to people in your team as your Fix Your Team plan progresses, to take care of their wellbeing. Your wellbeing matters just as much!

4. DEBRIEF, DEBRIEF, DEBRIEF

When handling conflict and complaints, it is essential that you debrief regularly. This is of fundamental importance in maintaining your own sense of balance and wellbeing.

A debrief is a semi-structured conversation in which you can talk about your experience, reflect on what has happened, gain some insights and learn from the experience. Debriefing may occur once or in a series of regular meetings, in a confidential setting. Debriefing can be formal (such as with a supervisor or colleague) or informal (such as with a friend or loved one).

Importantly, the purpose of a debrief is not to discuss the details of the dysfunction or people involved. The focus should be on your own emotional experience, not on rational problem-solving. Debriefing can prevent a build-up of stress and other negative emotion.

During a debrief, you may explore what you have experienced, and how you feel about the participants' conduct towards you. You can seek support and guidance on how to minimise the process impact on you. Debriefing may also allow you to receive insights and advice and to ask questions based on the experiences of the person you are debriefing with.

If debriefing within your organisation is not appropriate — because of issues of confidentiality, for instance — consider approaching an external professional, psychologist or coach.

As a final step, debrief at the end of the Fix Your Team plan to consider the process as a whole. Discussing what worked and what didn't will help improve the process, and it will build your wisdom and understanding too.

AS YOU SET OUT TO FIX YOUR TEAM ...

The members of a dysfunctional team may have lost sight of their ability to influence how the team works. Old habits, difficult times and personal challenges can make people fearful of trying new ways of being. Remember, you can *always* choose to create better ways of working together. While this may already be clear to you, and more so after reading this book, others in your team may not have had this necessary revelation. They may be clinging to old ways of working, which are defective but familiar. Understandably, it may take some people longer to trust each other to build new ways of working. Even the co-worker who understands the logic behind a proposed change may fear the unknown, or doubt that they can adapt in the ways the team expects of them.

Be compassionate with each other, recognising that your colleagues' preparedness to trust each other and work together to effect change has probably been damaged.

At the same time, do hold each other accountable. Make sure you stay in there for the long haul, because real and meaningful change can take time. Encourage one another, each and every day, to bring your best selves to work as you implement the Tools to Fix Your Team.

Fixing your team will take grit, kindness, moral courage and openness to be vulnerable. You'll have to stick your neck out. You'll need to be strategic. It will take some audacity to say: *We can be better than this! We deserve to work in a healthier, happier workplace! Together, we are able to make this team into a high-functioning, respected and high-achieving group of superstars!*

We wish you well, readers, as you go out and Fix Your Team to create a productive, cooperative, happy and meaningful workplace where you can all thrive.

In years to come, you will probably look back and know that Fixing Your Team was one of the toughest and most rewarding things you have done in your career. You took a stand, worked out what needed to change, and effected that change, for the good of everyone around you.

FIX YOUR TEAM

Toolkit

A quick way to find just the tools you need to fix specific team issues

FIX YOUR TEAM Toolkit

WHAT'S GOING ON?
Gossip culture

What might have started as harmless banter in the lunch room, or constructive speculation in challenging times, now has people delighting in others' misfortunes, true or fabricated. Gossip exists in many workplaces, and it can be destructive.

Read more about this dysfunction on page 3.

HOW TO FIX IT
Address unhealthy conflict

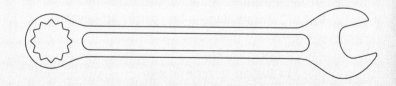

FIX YOUR TEAM Toolkit

Unprofessional conduct

When you're having a bad day, it can be difficult to mask your feelings and keep your negativity, anger, anxiety or frustrations to yourself. But when the bad days are causing hurt and disruption to other members of the team, and the accepted standards of behaviour are slipping, a nasty culture starts to develop.

Read more about this dysfunction on page 9.

Toxic Personalities

We've all been in a situation — in our family, friendship group or workplace — where one person seems to undermine everyone's enjoyment of good things that are going on, and exploits any opportunity to dampen the mood. They are the Bad Apple that can rot the whole barrel.

Read more about this dysfunction on page 17.

Personal crisis

We all have ups and downs, and sometimes people go through terrible challenges in their personal lives. This can make it very difficult for them to maintain a happy outlook and make a productive contribution at work.

Read more about this dysfunction on page 25.

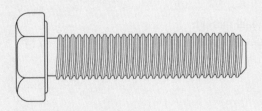

Workplace romance

Given the amount of time we all spend at work, it's not surprising that many of us will meet our romantic partner there. But if that relationship ends, strong negative emotions can surface leading to lower motivation and focus due to the grieving process, especially if their work places them in close proximity.

Read more about this dysfunction on page 33.

Note that this refers to two colleagues who have been in a consensual romantic or sexual relationship that has ended—not one person inappropriately pursuing a colleague, which is called sexual harassment.

Family ties

Nepotism means the use of power or influence to secure unfair workplace advantage for members of one's own family. An employee with a familial connection within the company will get ahead because of that connection, and not because they have special merit, skills or experience.

Read more about this dysfunction on page 39.

Develop the team's character and connections

Develop Leadership and Management

FIX YOUR TEAM Toolkit

Lack of diversity and inclusion

Having a team that is made up of the same type of people—mostly the same gender, age, ethnic background, religion and education—can go unnoticed. Employees can become victims of inequitable work practices when the people with power perceive them to be different, less worthy or more troublesome,

Read more about this dysfunction on page 47.

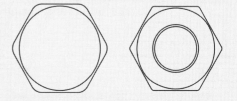

Unresolved historical issue

Simply put, there's an issue from the past (say, in the past two years) from which the team hasn't yet moved on. Whatever the issue was, it was significant enough to rock the foundations of how the team worked together.

Read more about this dysfunction on page 55.

Address unhealthy conflict

Develop the team's character and connections

Care for each other

Depending on the nature of the historic issue, you may require other tools such as:

The manager's style

We expect a lot of our managers, and when they fail to deliver, the backlash can be severe. They are often doing their best, but they lack the nous, the trust of their team or the support of the organisation to hear and fully comprehend how they are performing in their management role.

Read more about this dysfunction on page 63.

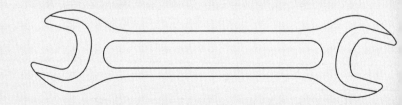

Unhealthy competition

Competition that is cooperative sees employees working together to achieve, making the team greater than the sum of its parts. Unhealthy competition pits employee against employee, with aggressive employees climbing over the top of their colleagues to get ahead, leaving frustration, insult and damage in their wake.

Read more about this dysfunction on page 71.

No clarity, no accountability

From an outsider's point of view, teams that operate in chaos may not appear to be dysfunctional. These teams often do achieve an acceptable level of output. The problem is they are achieving far less than they could if they were operating efficiently and with clarity of focus.

Read more about this dysfunction on page 79.

Align with values

Develop Leadership and Management

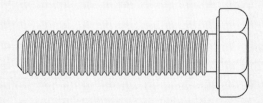

Overwork

Every team has peaks and troughs in workload to meet fluctuating demands. It becomes a problem when the whole team is under heavy strain for a sustained period of time, and there is no sign of the workload lessening and overwork and the consequent risk of employee burnout becoming more likely.

Read more about this dysfunction on page 87.

Align with values

Care for each other

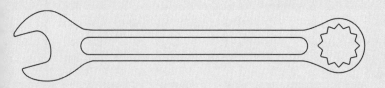

SELECT RESEARCH CITATIONS

Meeting your partner at work (page 33): Michael Rosenfeld and Reuben Thomas (2012), 'Searching for a Mate: The Rise of the Internet as a Social Intermediary', *American Sociological Review*, 77(4). See also Aziz Ansari with Eric Klinenberg, *Modern Romance* (2015).

Groupthink and the moral hazard of sameness (pages 52–3): Maria del Carmen Triana, Mevan Jayasinghe and Jenna Pierper (2015), 'Perceived workplace racial discrimination and its correlates: A meta-analysis', *Journal of Organizational Behaviour*, 36(4); see also Yin Paradies and Amanuel Elias, 'How racism and a lack of diversity can harm productivity in our workplaces', *The Conversation*, 28 February 2017.

Presenteeism/long hours (page 89): Svartedalens experiment reported by Rebecca Greenfield, 'The six-hour work day increases productivity. So will Britain and America adopt one?', *Independent*, 6 June 2016.

Overtime (page 90): David Baker, Molly Johnson and Richard Denniss (2014), *Walking the Tightrope: Have Australians achieved work/life balance?*, The Australia Institute; see also Tom Swann and Jim Stanford (2016), *Excessive Hours and Unpaid Overtime: An Update*, The Australia Institute.

Mindfulness (pages 160–2): Shian-Ling Keng, Moria Smoski and Clive Robins (2011), 'Effects of Mindfulness on Psychological Health: A Review of Empirical Studies', *Clinical Psychological Review*, 31(6), 1041–56.

Autonomy and job satisfaction (pages 162–4): Gensler (2013), *2013 U.S. Workplace Survey: Key Findings.*

Positive mindset and good achievement (page 164): Jeni Burnette, Ernest O'Boyle, Eric Vanepps, Jeffrey Pollack and Eli Finkel (2012), 'Mind-Sets Matter: A Meta-Analytic Review of Implicit Theories and Self-Regulation', *Psychological Bulletin*, 139.

The business case for diversity (page 173): Diversity Council Australia (Jane O'Leary and Andrew Legg), *DCA-Suncorp Inclusion@Work Index 2017–2018: Mapping the State of Inclusion in the Australian Workforce*, Sydney, Diversity Council Australia, 2017.

Inherent and acquired diversity of leaders (page 173): Sylvia Ann Hewlett, Melinda Marshall and Laura Sherbin, 'How Diversity Can Drive Innovation', *Harvard Business Review*, December 2013.

Implicit bias in recruitment (page 178): Stephen J Dubner and Steven Levitt (2009), *Freakonomics.*

Fraud detection by employee tip-offs (pages 187–8): Association of Certified Fraud Examiners (2014), *Report to the Nation on Occupational Fraud and Abuse.*

Making a formal complaint about misconduct (page 188): Victorian Public Sector Commission (2016), *Data Insights: Bullying in the Victorian Public Sector;* Anthony J Brown (ed) (2007), *Whistleblowing in the Australian Public Sector*, Griffith Law School.

Return to suitable work (page 212): The Royal Australasian College of Physicians (2010), *Australasian Faculty of Occupational and Environmental Medicine Position Statement 2010: Realising the Benefits of Work.*

Psychosocial triggers for aggression (page 242): See M. Sandy Hershcovis and others (2007), 'Predicting Workplace Aggression: A Meta-Analysis', *Journal of Applied Psychology*, 92(1), 228-238.

INDEX

MOOSKI

A Delightful Workplace Experience

Mooski is a three-week online program for teams. In Mooski, colleagues get to know each other better, reflect as individuals on their traits, values, work relationships and strengths, and apply those insights to their team.

 Based on the latest research from psychologists and business school experts, Mooski increases resilience, motivation, innovation, efficiency and happiness.

 Mooski is open to everyone, of all ages, abilities and learning styles. The messages include animation and podcasts, self-reflection, tasks in pairs and tasks across teams.

 Delivered via email and smartphone-friendly, Mooski is accessible anywhere in the world. Remote, home-based, flexible and shift workers can all participate.

 Mooski is low-cost, modern and enjoyable. Participants can immediately apply the learning in their day-to-day work. Easy!

Learn more and get Mooski for your team at
www.mooski.com.au

WORKLOGIC

Worklogic helps employers to promote positive workplace behaviour, and to resolve conflict and complaints fairly and respectfully. We have delivered over 1,500 projects since 2007 for employers large and small across Australia.

Worklogic can help you to Fix Your Team by:

- conducting a **FYT Team Review** of dysfunctional teams at your workplace
- **coaching** you to apply the FYT Toolkit to resolve team dysfunction
- **organising FYT Workshops to upskill your managers**
- **investigating** cases of misconduct or unprofessional behaviour
- running a **mediation** between disputing employees
- facilitating organisation **values projects**

Now that you have read *Fix Your Team*, **stay connected with us!**

You can receive free advice, the FYT workbook and invitations to events, webinars and workshops by the Worklogic team by signing up at **www.fix-your-team.com**

www.worklogic.com.au